to
Betty with
great respect
from H. Dundricu
Dec 3/2002

SURVIVING THE STORMS
MEMORY OF STALIN'S TYRANNY

by
Helen Dmitriew

translated by
Cathleen A. McClintic
and
George Mendez G.

The Press
at
California State University, Fresno

Library of Congress Catalog Card Number: 92-62075

Printed in the United States of America.

Managing Editor: Carla Jean Millar

Orders should be addressed to:

The Press at California State University, Fresno
Fresno, CA 93740-0096

To my beloved daughter Ena-Anna,
who shared with me all the horrors of war, hunger,
cold, and poverty, I dedicate this book.

It was a time when only the dead smiled,
happy for the tranquility . . .

Anna Akhmatova, *Requiem*

CONTENTS

From the Author

It is difficult to comprehend and describe the road along which I and millions of others like me traveled. It was a route filled with hunger, cold, illnesses, and outrages.

The aim of my book is to give an account of the past, which I remember with pain, and of the patience and strength that have helped me to endure the humiliation and fear. I have tried to recall the horror of the dictatorship that brought destruction to our country and death to millions of innocent people. I want to share with the reader my impressions of the life I have lived so that people know a fraction of the truth about the terrible reign of brutality. This is the cry of an aching heart, tormented by pain.

I have thought it necessary to change my relatives' names.

I believe in a better future for my homeland and hope to see the Russian people completely free of the fetters of communism.

This book was written in Russian. The translation into English was done by my former students, Cathleen McClintic and George Mendez G. To them I express my deep gratitude for their work. I would also like to thank Terry A. Cain and Wendy Costa for editing the completed manuscript.

TRANSLATORS' NOTE

As is common usage with many Russian speakers, there are many diminutive forms of address throughout this book. Most of these have not been explained in notes, for often the name may be determined from the root. For example, Elena becomes Lena, Lenok, Lenochka, or Lenusenka.

Proverbs have been translated from Russian into English in cases where the English equivalent very closely approximates the original in both language and spirit. Otherwise a note has been provided. The intent has not been to transform this work into an English one, but to retain those peculiarly Russian turns of phrase that give life and reality to the words of the author.

CHAPTER ONE

JOURNEY THROUGH TORMENT

1

I was the youngest in my family, a spoiled, capricious little girl. Everything had to be just as I wanted it. Both my parents loved me, but I was especially my father's favorite. I resembled him physically and temperamentally. My mother, a calm, self-possessed woman, especially adored her first-born, Boris. She taught him to read when he was four and instilled in him a love for books. In childhood he demonstrated an aptitude in his studies that made both our parents proud. Marina, my older sister, was a beauty. My mother had borne six children, but three had died early, leaving an incurable wound in her heart.

Mother always gave us a lot of her time and attention. She taught us to read and write even before we went to school, and I still remember the verses, fairy tales, and songs she taught us. Her gentleness, her devotion to the family, and her values forever guided us all. My mother was a sensitive, devoted wife and a loving mother.

In contrast, my father was very jealous, especially when he had been drinking. Mother patiently heard him out and, in a gentle voice, tried to calm him. There was no reason for his jealousy, especially since he himself was probably not very faithful to his wife on his extended business trips.

My parents were very good-looking. Father was tall and well-proportioned with fair hair and blue eyes. Mother was of medium height with beautiful, regular facial features. She wore her hair up and was always neat and elegant.

When he was younger, my father was not as interested in business matters as he was in continuing his education. His dreams went unrealized, however. He had married early and, due to the deaths of his older brother in World War I and his father on the very day I was born in 1916, took charge of the family's affairs.

Both my parents strove to provide all their children with an education. From secondary school on, Boris and Marina lived and attended school in the city. I expected to follow them when I was old enough.

Father worked at the cooperative and traveled all around the *oblast'*.[1] He was often away from the family for five or six months at a time. When he returned home, it was a real holiday for everyone.

After the Revolution and the Civil War, there were quite a few orphans and destitute women, whose fathers and husbands had been lost in the war or shot by the Bolsheviks. Besides their own children, my parents cared for four orphans—two boys and two girls—whom my father had brought home from different *raiony*.[2] My parents firmly believed that one should be sensitive to those who have suffered so much. These adopted children called my parents "Mama" and "Papa," just as I did.

During the 1920s, we didn't feel material difficulties as much as others, since my father was able to obtain the necessities through the cooperative. The majority of the population, however, experienced great shortages during these years. World War I, the Revolution, the Civil War, and the Bolsheviks' rise to power all contributed to the ruin of our country's economy and doomed our people to terrible poverty.

Seeing their system being destroyed, the Bolsheviks in 1924 had introduced the New Economic Policy (NEP)—a turn toward capitalism. In a short time, small businesses made great progress, yet a change for the worse came again after Lenin's death and Stalin's subsequent rise to power. He put an end to NEP in 1929 and began forced collectivization. The destruction of the better peasant workers began in the villages; the slogan was "Destroy the Kulaks as a Class." At the same time, reprisals began against the owners of small businesses, and the government imposed back-breaking taxes on private businesses and on peasants who did not want to enter the collective farms.[3] Stalin's government made increasingly harsh demands on its people in its quest to achieve socialism. No one was immune.

The four adopted orphans were already married and on their own by this time. Only I remained at home with my parents: Boris and Marina were still away at school. My father tried to accomplish all that the Soviet regime demanded of him, but this was a very difficult task, and horses were his weakness. During NEP he had bought some purebred horses, which we all learned to ride. When the government tax was imposed, he had to sell all his horses, but the proceeds were enough for only a small part of the amount due. "Representatives" of the local government soon visited our house and threatened my father. My mother and I heard this exchange and were filled with dread. We sensed something terrible was going to happen but had no conception of the atrocities that awaited.

My father came home gloomy more and more frequently and spoke with my mother in hushed tones. From the isolated sentences I sometimes caught while trying to listen to their conversations, it was clear that Mother was trying to persuade Father to flee our home and hide from persecution. He objected strongly and told her that he would not leave his family defenseless.

"You say to disappear, but then what?" he once responded to her plea. "We live in such a time that no decent man can avoid prison or, even worse, death. No . . . I will go nowhere. I will await what comes."

Mother cried. That conversation made me even more frightened, and I began to wake up at night, alert to every sound.

As May 1929 came to an end, fear gripped the land. Menace hung like a dark cloud over every house. Then the arrests began. People began to shun one another and even ceased speaking aloud. Relatives stopped calling on family members. The people in the community of Yasvino hoped that if others were arrested perhaps they would be spared this awful fate. Young people scattered to hide from persecution, while their elders began to vanish into the torture chambers of the authorities. Even those who sang in the church choir fell into disfavor.

I do not remember the exact date when my father, who was a salesman for the cooperative, was summoned to the local trade union committee, and I do not know what happened to him there. When he returned home and told Mother about it, I could tell that our comfortable family life had come to an end. I watched as he solemnly removed his wedding ring and handed it to Mother. They had been married twenty-three years, and the ring had never been off his finger.

Neither my father nor mother undressed or went to bed that evening. I lay in bed and listened to the quiet tick of the clock on the wall. It struck twelve midnight. Suddenly, heavy steps sounded around the house, followed by a knock on the front door. Father went to open the door. Mother clutched his arm and begged him to run away through another door. The knocks became more insistent and were accompanied by swearing. Father opened the door and six members of the Cheka burst into the house.[4]

"Citizen Petrov?"

"Yes, that's me," answered Father.

"You are under arrest!"

Father did not reply or question them. I glimpsed his pale face as he hugged me tightly. "My little daughter," he whispered to me. "I am not a criminal. I have been an honest man and have taught all of you to be good people. No matter what happens to me, you never need be ashamed of your own father."

Meanwhile, the men were searching the house, turning everything upside-down. As they threw down all the plates from the shelves in the kitchen, Mother stood and wept quietly. But when one of the men grabbed Father by the arm and dragged him toward the door, she flung herself at his captor, screaming, "Why?" He shoved her aside roughly without answering.

The door slammed shut and we both looked through the window at my departing father. Outside, dogs howled, portending a yet more troubled time to come. Mother sobbed for a long time after they took Father away, her mournful sounds reminding me of a wounded bird fighting its last skirmish with death.

The next morning, we learned that ten men had been arrested.

After my father was arrested, everything fell to my mother, but she wasn't able to do anything but cry. I felt helpless; I didn't know how to approach her or how to calm her. My father had been the head of the family for some time. His mother, Grandma Elena, was still alive and came to us, but was unable to speak through her tears. Although Mother had older brothers and sisters, her parents had died long before.

Ten long days passed after my father's arrest. Mother walked sleeplessly about the house at night from one window to another. I was also unable to sleep. Suddenly, on the eleventh night, I saw my mother move and heard footsteps at the front door. A loud knock pierced the silence. "Open up!" came the rude command.

She hurried to the door and drew back the bolt. At the door were local "representatives," former hooligans who destroyed honest workers, beat defenseless women, and cast small children out into the street. They were fully supported by the higher authorities, who were similar in character. Two of the men at the door had been idle drunkards in the past, but now they were "the law."

They came to search our home and proceeded to confiscate all our property. Family portraits crashed to the floor, and the wallpaper in the kitchen soon lay in shreds. One of the representatives demanded Mother's wedding rings. She removed Father's ring, but was unable to remove her own. He grabbed her hand and pulled off the ring. Blood flowed from Mother's hand: the skin on the middle of her finger over the joint was badly torn. More people appeared at the house and began to carry away all our possessions.

Then the leader of the group announced that we were under arrest. They took us out into the street, where we joined other such victims, who were already in carts. We recognized these people as the families of the ten men who had been arrested the same night as Father. We were taken in an unknown direction, under guard. Mother hadn't thought to take along any of the most basic necessities.

We traveled a whole day, and it was quite late when we arrived at an assembly location, not far from the city of Roslavl'. Our captors, heartless and brutal men, herded us to a bathhouse and into a disinfection chamber. When they turned on the disinfection gas, people choked from the clouds of acrid vapor.

All these elaborate arrangements had been prepared earlier by the authorities. They were not concerned with feeding a starving population, but, with their special wisdom, had orchestrated a means to destroy the best workers.

Our group, comprised of women, children, and old people, remained at this site in hastily constructed barracks. On the third evening we noticed a column of people moving toward us from an open field. We could not distinguish who these people were until someone cried out that they were our arrested fathers. Guards were driving them on foot from the prison like cattle. The authorities halted them a short distance from us and ordered them to sit on the ground. The men remained seated for about two hours, until finally they were herded to our barracks. The men all looked awful: unshaven, unwashed, with expressions of untold horror on their faces.

The thirteen days of separation and uncertainty had seemed like thirteen years. No one knew what lay in the future. A terrible feeling of helplessness and grief weighed upon all of us, but my mother and I were overjoyed to be reunited with my father.

Father threw himself at us and hugged us both tightly, unable to speak. For the first time I saw tears in his eyes. This reunion has remained forever in my memory.

The authorities began to divide the arrested people into groups. Some prisoners managed to avoid the fate that later befell us by bribing the guards with valuables concealed on their persons. As we later learned, those who had these valuables prolonged their own lives and were able to flee, although no one knew for how long. My own parents were so frightened by the desperate situation that they didn't even think to offer a bribe. Instead they submitted to a fate that turned out to be cruel beyond comprehension.

Each day we were fed some kind of unrecognizable slop and given one piece of bread each. Early one morning, after having been held for two weeks in this transit camp, we were loaded onto a freight train and taken away to an unknown destination. The cars were packed with people, and the small windows below the roof of the car were covered with barbed wire. Because of his job as a traveling salesman, my father knew the rail lines well and said we were being taken in an eastward direction toward Siberia. It is impossible to convey in words what went on in the hearts of these doomed people who were guilty of nothing.

The door of the car was opened only when we were given our daily ration of bread, so there was no fresh air to breathe. There was neither drinking water nor toilets. The women looked after the small children, who cried incessantly. One woman managed to put her hand through a small window and pour out her children's waste onto the head of a guard, who fired his weapon upward and screamed horribly foul things at all of us. "I will shoot all of you like dogs . . . !" Following these threats were vulgar words that to this day I am unable to repeat aloud.

The commandant of the train was an NKVD officer (we did not know their names, of course).[5] He ordered the cars to be opened at a few of the stops. The train was halted not at the stations, but at sidings far from witnesses of these outrages of Stalinist tyranny.

After we passed Smolensk, the detachment of guards was replaced by different NKVDists. The new commander fulfilled his duties "masterfully." He was a beast in the form of a man. Every spoken word was accompanied by a profanity. His coarse, barbaric behavior was directed not only toward us, but also toward the guards who were his subordinates.

We all lost our sense of time and had no idea what day of the week it was. Since a gloomy twilight reigned in the car even during the day, it seemed that a continuous night had fallen.

Several weeks had passed when we arrived at Omsk one night. Everyone was ordered out of the cars and arranged into rows. Parents carried their sleeping children, whose hoarse cries punctuated the cold as they awoke. Their mothers cried with them.

Like cattle, we were all driven to a bathhouse. Everything had been provided for us by the "builders of the new life." Even these so-called baths were specially equipped for the exiles. We were taken into the corridor in groups. Everyone had to remove all clothing and hand it to the authorities for disinfection. We passed in formation through a cold shower. There was no soap whatsoever. I will never forget the sound: not simple cries, but a continuous howl from the children and women. The men were, of course, separated from our group.

At the exit on the other end of the bath, we had to try to retrieve our own stinking clothing. No numbers had been given out for the clothing and it was impossible to locate our own things. People grabbed what they could so as not to be left completely naked. All the while, there was no end to the sobbing of the victims and cursing by their captors.

Following our "bath," we were organized once again into rows and herded onto the train. Not surprisingly, by this time the majority of children had become ill and had to be carried in their mothers' arms. Our train went on again at a slow speed. We were on the road another week. They had already thrown many dead from the cars. I don't think they were even buried, but simply tossed down the railroad embankments.

At last, more dead than alive, we arrived at the Siberian city of Prokop'evsk, where coal mining is concentrated. They unloaded the cars and drove us on foot through the outskirts of the city to a camp that had been "prepared" for us. The name of this camp, Birch Grove, was itself an irony and mockery. Not only were there no birch trees, but there was not even a single blade of green grass anywhere. Instead, a thick layer of black coal dust covered the soil. When the wind blew, the black dust was stirred up in big noxious clouds, making it difficult to breathe.

The camp was composed of various nationalities. The majority were Russian, but there were also Ukrainians, Byelorussians, Uzbeks, Tatars, Bashkirs, Kirghiz, and many other national minorities. They did not separate the inhabitants of the camp by nationality, so it was possible to hear pain, suffering, and torment in various languages. This was my first experience with different people and their customs.

A commandant ruled in every barrack. Everything, from the distribution of bread to the assignment of work, passed through his hands. The men were sent to work in the coal mines. The women and adolescents were assigned field work, leaving the younger children to fend for themselves.

Typhus and dysentery raged through the camp. Like houseflies in the first fall frost, people died and the larger families quickly grew smaller. Although many adults died, children were the first victims. At first there were about 350 children in the camp. After several months only eight of us remained. I will always remember with bitter irony a slogan of the day: "Thanks to Comrade Stalin for a happy childhood."

I remember especially one Ukrainian family that originally consisted of twelve people: father, mother, their son, his wife, and eight children. The oldest child, sixteen years old, was the first to die, followed by the grandmother and then the children, one after another. The father died last. The final days of his life were horrible. He gave off a horrible stench and looked like a walking corpse.

One day he walked up to a stove that had been placed outside near the barracks. A woman was baking pancakes from rotten potatoes. He focused on it with a wild gaze, grabbed a hot potato pancake, swallowed it in an instant, and immediately fell down dead. His corpse lay by the stove for four days, his face and open mouth covered by a swarm of flies. No one had the strength to move his corpse away from the stove. When his own parents, children, and wife had died, the man had somehow managed to bury them, but there was no one to bury him.

Toward winter, those of us who remained alive were transferred to other barracks. These were also wooden, but inside there were signs that they had once been plastered. There were holes in the corners of the barracks large enough to put one's head through and bedbugs and lice everywhere.

The commandant of the entire camp was a veritable monster named Khrolov. In the eyes of the authorities, he had characteristics especially suited to deal mercilessly with prisoners such as us, the "enemies of the people."

Sometimes a scenario such as this was arranged near the commandant's office: a barrel of moldy, completely decomposed herring would be brought out, and food distribution would begin. The prisoners, having lost their senses from deprivation and the bitter cold, would fall on it in disorder, pushing and shoving one another. At this time Khrolov, mounted on a horse, would plunge into the crowd and flog heads and arms with his lash. Since it was plaited of leather and wire, his strokes would cut faces and arms until they were covered with blood. He took great pleasure from these activities.

My father worked in the mine, taking his bread ration with him. He told me how the men would fall down from exhaustion in the mines and how guards beat the horses, which had gone blind from working without light. These poorly fed horses were harnessed to large trailers of coal. My father and I were both horse lovers, so I was unable to listen to his stories without tears. When they brought the dead horses out of the mines, they would throw them into an open field, on top of a thick layer of human waste that had been removed from the city latrines. The Kirghiz somehow managed to creep through the barbed wire obstructions and, like ravens, cut the flesh from the softer parts of the dead horses.[6] They wore black clothing, black headgear, and narrow black casings around the plaits of their braided hair. They were not talkative, but I often heard the phrase *Kil' manda? Kil' manda?* Someone told me that this means "What is to come?" We were all asking ourselves that question.

The Slavs exchanged scant phrases among themselves. The Muslims tried to keep somewhat farther away from us, sensing antagonism. Different languages and different traditions separated us, but we all expected the same fate: death.

The onerous days dragged slowly by. Hard frosts, snowstorms, and snowdrifts came. Even though this was the heart of the Soviet coal mining industry, we were given no coal or anything else with which to fuel the stoves. We had to stand in line in the bitter cold to get what little water there was, and when the water pipe froze and burst we went completely without. We tried to melt snow, especially right after a storm. When a strong wind blew, however, the fresh, clean snow would become mixed with coal dust and make the water dirty and smelly.

That fall my father began to cough up blood, and it became difficult for him to walk. He finally just lay in bed, answering Mother's and my questions with nods. He never complained about the pain in his chest or about the hunger and cold. He blamed himself for our situation, since he had not listened to my mother's pleadings to hide from his persecutors. He still hoped for justice, although there was no apparent source from which to expect it.

My mother lost many of her teeth, blood oozed from her gums, and her hair fell out, but she tried to stay on her feet. One day she took our rags to wash. (It was not possible to call these rags linens.) Laundering in the cold, dirty water, she got a blister that burst and became infected. After two days her whole arm, almost to the shoulder, had become red and swollen. The swelling progressed, and she developed a high temperature. She began to lose consciousness periodically and to rave.

"What can I do?" I thought. Although I was still on my feet, there was no end to my despair. Two Byelorussian Catholics, an old man and his son who also worked in the mine, lived around the corner next to our room. Seeing my helplessness, the old man told me that a few kilometers from our camp was a colony of specialists from Germany and Czechoslovakia. These specialists were people who had been sympathetic to communism while living in their own countries. They had been lured to the Soviet Union by promises of an "earthly paradise." In developing the mining industry, the Soviet Union used its own people as slaves and the Germans and Czechs as specialists.

Compared to Soviet standards, foreign specialists enjoyed good living conditions in comfortable apartments with parquet floors, toilets, and indoor plumbing. Special distribution stores, stocked with better clothing and food, were opened for them. The frozen corpses of our people lay near the fences of the specialists' colony.

The majority of these foreign specialists were Catholics, and they were sympathetic to the old Byelorussian when he made his way through their settlement. Since he was Catholic, he knew how to address these religious people: "Glory to the Most Holy Virgin."

Seeing my grief and helplessness, he advised me to go to this settlement, which I did. Snowdrifts rose as high as the roofs of the barracks, so it was easy to climb out and leave the camp. On the way to the settlement I thought, "This is a deception, for I am Orthodox." Coming to the conclusion that it was possible to praise God in any language, however, I set out on my trip for a piece of bread.

My first attempt ended in failure. I received nothing when I knocked on doors. The answer was the same everywhere: "Go away from here." The second time I decided to repeat the sentence that the old man had taught me, as I saw no other way out. The results were positive. Several of the settlement's dwellers asked me questions regarding my parents, how old I was, and where I was from. They gave me pieces of white bread and sometimes even soup in a tin can. They began to call me to clean floors, take dogs for walks, and carry firewood and coal from the street into the apartments. In this way I began to obtain sustenance for my sick parents. When I brought food I would sit on my parents' plank bed and feed them in turn. They lay in bed, covered by sheepskins, which were alive with lice and bedbugs.

After eight months of illness and my diligent nursing, my father was the first to lift his head slightly and then, with my help, to get up from the bed. While my father began to move about slowly, my mother was still almost motionless. The swelling on her whole left arm did not go away. The little bones of the wrist joint fell out of the open wound, completely rotted, as if pierced by needles. Pus oozed from the wound all the time. Her arm was totally paralyzed. My mother did not possess as much will power as my father, but his example was contagious. She saw how I struggled to save them and how my father added all his efforts. This gave her the desire to live. Sometimes she said in a quiet voice, "I don't want to leave you, my dear ones; pray for me." I prayed fervently, often on my knees, swollen from rheumatism.

I have retained images of my sick parents and of other people's deaths all my life. These images have made me stoic and persistent, as well as sensitive to others' grief, and a helper to others when possible. Unfortunately, misfortune and struggle are the best school in which to refine one's feelings. Looking back, remembering all the unbearable horror, the question thrusts itself on me: "How could we bear all this and remain alive?" My answer is that from childhood my mother and grandmother Elena had infused in me a deep belief in God. I prayed in my own words, asking God to save all of us from the grave. Our captivity taught me how infinitely dear life is, no matter how difficult circumstances are.

2

In 1932, the ranks of the exiles grew thinner and thinner. Already I could not find anyone who had been with us on the train to Siberia. There seemed no way out except for the most horrible one—death.

We tried to drive this thought from our minds. We began to speak more often of how to save ourselves from death. At one such family conference we decided that Father should try to escape from the camp. The guard was not so diligent now, because the authorities did not believe the walking dead could go very far.

One dark night my father crept to the barbed wire fence, crawled through to the other side, and disappeared into the darkness. I did not know what became of him after that for many years.

After several months, I tried to persuade my mother to escape as well. She feared reprisals if they caught us and wondered if she had sufficient strength. Risk is a noble thing, however, and we set off on the road before sunrise on an early spring morning. We knew neither the direction we were going nor our final destination. We had to go by back roads, to avoid the arm of the law and the defenders of socialism. We walked for a long time through the taiga. Had we not been so sick, frightened, and hungry, we might have been able to appreciate the beauty of nature and the riches of the forest.

The lack of vitamins gave me a progressing case of scurvy, and Mother lost the rest of her teeth. One day we came across a hamlet in the taiga that the authorities apparently did not know about. It was a community of Baptists. While sitting at the table, they prayed aloud freely, which surprised me. At home, we were not to utter the name of God aloud.

We didn't know how many were in the group or the name of this village. They were involved in agriculture and grew rye in a large clearing in the forest. Around the huts were vegetable gardens. They fed us, and we slept on the enclosed porch of a hut. Their relations with us were cool because we were Orthodox. Nevertheless, we spent about a week there. Having rested and grown a little stronger, we set out again into the unknown.

In the taiga we found a plant similar in taste to garlic and ate its green, oblong leaves. The vitamins and minerals strengthened my gums, and less blood oozed from them. We also gathered various kinds of berries.

It was easy to lose your way in the taiga, especially without clear bearings for north and south. We tried to go along the edge of the forest. The population in this area was very sparse, although we sometimes met traveling hunters who taught us how to avoid wild animals. Bears were especially dangerous, and we had to shout all the time to scare them off.

We lost track of how long we wandered through this part of the countryside. We distinguished only day and night and did not know what day of the week it was or even what month. We had neither the physical nor mental strength to care about time. We were not certain when we would reach the European part of the country or whether we would even reach it at all.

Moving away from the taiga, we came to a fertile region adjacent to small rivers, which was marshy in areas. We concluded we were nearing the Irtysh River. Soon we came upon a *kolkhoz* village.[7] The peasants were not as frightened as in the central part of the Soviet Union, since their distance from Soviet authorities made them more cheerful and assured.

My mother walked through the village to obtain some pieces of bread. In one hut a peasant woman asked if I could stay with her child for a little while. She had three children; the youngest girl was nine months old. She took us to the bathhouse and heated us baths. Fortunately it was Saturday, the traditional bath day. So that we would be cleanly dressed, she gave us something in the way of clothing, and she cut my hair. She then fed us black rye bread with a piece of salt pork.

The pork and rye bread were too heavy for our stomachs, which had not seen real food for ages, and our bodies were exhausted. We both fell ill, and it took us several days to recover. We lived for some time with this kind woman. We did not ask her and she did not tell us where her husband was, but he was not at home while we were there. Curious neighbors soon began to inquire who we were, where we were going, and where we were from. It was clear we had to begin our trek again. The woman showed us the direction to the next village and we set out.

We reached the village and were walking down a street when a huge dog suddenly broke its chain and lunged at us. It pounced on my mother, mauling her bad arm. The dog's master barely fared better as he dragged the beast away. He took us into his house, asked that we tell no one about the occurrence, and promised to take us to the nearest station, sixty kilometers away.

By that evening, however, my mother had developed a high temperature. Her bad arm was covered with open wounds. I did not leave her side and prayed, asking God not to take her from me. She was all I had left; my father's whereabouts (or whether he had even survived his escape) were still unknown. I tried to speak to Mother, but she was unconscious and could not answer. Two and a half weeks passed.

While on my knees in front of her, I suddenly felt the touch of her right hand on my head. She strained to say something, but it was only disconnected words. Later she asked me where she was. Thanking God, I was ecstatic that once again I was able to hear the voice of the person dearest to me. Other people, no matter how likable and kind, were still strangers. Hearing my mother's feeble words was as if an angel from heaven spoke.

As I looked softly at her, I thought of what a remarkable woman she was. Mother had been unlucky from her youth. Parental objections did not permit her to marry the man she first loved, but instead forced her to enter an arranged union with my father. She poured love over us children, perhaps all the time remembering her broken dreams.

We very seldom heard her voice raised. She quietly conducted all the household affairs and brought us up with equal devotion. Often we children would fight, sometimes even coming to blows in Mother's absence. When we complained to her by turn, she patiently heard us out and admonished us not to quarrel. "There may come a time when you will regret what you are doing now," she once said. "There will be a time when you will want to see each other and will not be able." What a truthful prediction! I did not know whether my brother and sister were alive.

Images of the past played in my mind as I knelt in front of my mother, who lay on the straw, dying in a strange land. "Oh, no, I won't let you go, Mamochka! You cannot abandon me here alone, unneeded by anyone, ragged and ill."

I spoke continuously to her in these weeks, but I do not know whether she heard or understood my words. When at last she began to open her eyes periodically and speak short sentences, I started to have real hope that she would survive. As soon as she got up, the dog's master insisted we leave his house. He had forgotten his promise to take us to the station. Once again, we began to wander along the unfamiliar roads. Where were we going? Who needed us? What waited in the future? We could not foresee our fate.

The fear that we would be stopped by the authorities and asked for documents did not leave us for a minute. Fortunately, we gave the impression of being beggars rather than escapees from a concentration camp. We survived on the pieces of bread we got from peasants and often spent the night in a ravine, under a tree, or in the bushes. We were starving and shivering from the cold.

I don't know how many months passed before we eventually reached the Bolotnaia station, not far from Novosibirsk. Acquaintances of my parents lived somewhere near this station, but without their address we did not know how to find them. My maternal uncle Vasilii, who was also my godfather, lived in Novosibirsk and worked as an engineer in a factory, but Mother did not remember his address either.

We moved aimlessly along the streets. The rheumatism in my leg joints caused them to swell even more. The gnawing pain tormented me. We made our way quietly along the wooden sidewalk. My mother carried a small sack on her back, filled with pieces of stale bread and several rags imitating clothing. People took note of us, following us with suspicious glances. Since people of all classes were in flight from one place to another, the sight of a mother and daughter struggling down the street was not a curiosity. The streets of the cities were full of urki.[8] Many urki were originally from good families but had become homeless as they attempted to cover all traces of their pasts. Many of their parents had been shot in the first days of the Bolsheviks' arrival to power.

Distant relations, the Smirnov family, also lived at the Bolotnaia station, but my parents had never corresponded with them. Lowering our heads, we moved along, not daring to ask anyone about the Smirnovs. It would have been ridiculous to ask. On the corner of one street we noticed a woman on a porch, shaking out a rug. We didn't have the strength to continue our journey. As we approached the gate to the house, the woman began to look at us attentively. "Mamochka, ask this woman," I suggested desperately. "Maybe she knows about the Smirnovs."

The woman could not have recognized Mother, now a crippled woman without teeth, who looked ninety years old. She had a dirty kerchief on her head and wore baggy, ill-fitting clothing. The woman had never even seen me. Suddenly my mother stopped, gasped, and exclaimed, "Liuda! Is that really you?"

The woman became even more serious. "Who are you?" she asked.

"It is a miracle of God," continued Mother. "Do you really not know me, Liudochka? I'm Tat'iana, remember me?"

"Tania, my dear! How could I not remember how we always played together and shared secrets."

They hugged while I stood by and watched as they cried and exchanged questions. Mother pointed at me, emphasizing that I was her daughter, a martyr who saved her life.

Liudmilla Smirnov invited us into her home. The house was new. Her husband worked for the railroad. Railroad workers, like miners, were specialists who had privileges. They did not live in luxury but were in a much more comfortable position than other people. Their house was clean and orderly. It felt strange to sit down on chairs in a kitchen. We were dirty and ragged with thousands of lice.

"I will heat water and bring a basin so that you both can bathe," said Liudmilla. "And I'll give you some clothing . . . yours needs to be burned."

Liudmilla then cut my hair. With very short hair and sunken eyes, my body looked deformed. My skin stretched tightly over bone, my joints were swollen, and my back was covered with itching wounds. She gave me some of her daughter's clothing, which was too large for me, but it was wonderful to feel clean clothing on my body.

At first she tried not to ask questions, but then said that she had heard about our plight from relatives. She said that no one ever expected to see us alive again, since rumor had it that we had perished. Just having us at her table put her at risk, for if the authorities discovered she was helping two runaways her whole family would suffer. Nevertheless, Liudmilla was exceedingly affectionate and helpful to us.

The Smirnovs had two children. Their adult daughter had graduated with a degree in chemistry and worked in that field. Their son was still studying at the institute. We learned from Liudmilla that her husband would not be home for several days. Only God knew how her husband would react when he found out who we were and where we had come from, so we had to leave before his return. Liudmilla didn't say so, but we understood that if brothers and sisters or sons and daughters turned away those who had been arrested it was a mistake to expect intercession from distant relatives.

Liudmilla offered my mother forty rubles, which was all the money she had to give. We were boundlessly thankful that she had sheltered us for several days. She talked us out of going to Novosibirsk in search of my uncle Vasilii. He had a good job and four children, and our arrival on his doorstep could ruin him and destroy his comparatively peaceful life. Leaving Liudmilla's home, we felt ourselves fortified by food and family and, above all, by being clean and in more decent clothing.

We needed to make a decision on where to go. "Into God's world," said Mother. She was a very religious woman, more conservative in outlook than my father. She had been raised in a strict family, and this told in each step of her life. Gentleness and patience were distinctive features of her character.

She never complained of the pain or suffering, and her quiet tone was a positive and calming force on me. On the road she spoke little with me, but if we talked she tried to say something comforting, words that promised a better future.

We eventually decided to head for Novosibirsk but bypassed it unintentionally and found ourselves in the city of Barnaul. Our greatest problem was asking directions; we feared our own shadows, as they say. It was hard to trust strangers since there were secret informers everywhere. Sometimes, however, we could not avoid asking questions. We knocked at a small house located on the edge of Barnaul. A woman opened the door, and, having heard our story, invited us to come in. Her husband worked at the chemical plant. She began to ask us questions, and her sympathy for us was evident.

"But why Barnaul?" she asked.

"By pure chance," answered my mother.

She described our adventure at one rail station. We were so tired we could only crawl, so we climbed into one of the empty passenger cars sitting on the siding and hid under the seats to escape the wind. As we rested, I asked in alarm,

"Mamochka, what if the train carries us back again to where we came from?"

"Let it carry us where it pleases," she answered. "I can't move anymore."

The next morning the locomotive was connected to the rail cars and people began to board. When the passengers entered our car, they stowed their hand luggage under the seats before sitting down, which gave us away. A passenger informed the conductors, who dragged us both out and threw us off the car at the next station. We were still thankful that we had ridden at least a little way.

Having heard all this, our new acquaintance understood how we came to arrive in Barnaul.

3

The notion of riding on trains for a distance appealed to us, and after that first experience we often put the idea into practice. We tried to remain near the railroad all the time, and only one obstacle stood in our way: the railroad bridges, which were guarded by soldiers who could detain us. Our destination, always in our dreams, was Sverdlovsk, since from there it would be easier to find our way to our own region—the European part of Russia. Although physically we were completely exhausted, our spirit did not surrender. We resolved to die on the road if necessary, but not to abandon our dream.

We walked many more months to reach Sverdlovsk. The calluses on the soles of our feet burned as if they were on fire. Several times we managed to sneak onto freight trains or even onto open flatcars. We often rode until they caught us and threw us off the train. We learned from practice how to conceal ourselves in the general flow of the crowd at the stations. It was possible to spend the night sitting on the floor, because the trains were sometimes late by eight hours or more. Some passengers were detained at terminals for days at a time.

At long last, we reached the outskirts of Sverdlovsk

on foot and asked directions to the railroad terminal. It seemed such a distance! The last steps seemed the longest of all our journey. Compared to the distance we had traveled, it seemed that it shouldn't be so far to walk to the terminal in Sverdlovsk. Indeed, we had been on the road a year. I was about to turn fourteen.

When we finally crawled up to the Sverdlovsk terminal, we were struck by the many sounds and languages of the people. Some were "passengers" like us in the station, and the third-class waiting hall was packed, with people sitting on the floor, some even lying down. Ironically in this "classless society" there were separate waiting halls for third-, second-, and first-class passengers. Where was Soviet justice? Had this word been thrown out of the Soviet vocabulary? The Soviet elite evidently didn't want to mix with the innumerable dirty, simple toilers and homeless fugitives.

There was a square in front of the terminal, and people were sitting on the pavement. We joined them. Our hunger was unbearable. I got up and went to the buffet, which displayed sandwiches and pastries under glass. The people with money were drinking beer and lemonade and eating sandwiches. We hadn't even a kopek, so I couldn't buy anything.

Perhaps my appearance spoke for itself and attracted attention, because a tall, handsome man of about forty-five soon walked toward me. He was impeccably dressed in a dark gray suit and black patent leather shoes.

"Are you hungry, child?" he asked me.

As I looked at him, fear enveloped me, and I answered in a trembling voice, "No, I'm not hungry."

"That's not true. You want to eat," he objected, looking me straight in the eye. "Where are you going on the train?"

"I'm not riding, but walking."

"Are you alone or with your parents?" he continued.

My hands and legs began to tremble. "Why is he so interested in me?" I thought. "He's probably a Chekist."

"My mother is with me," I answered, after some hesitation.

"And where is she?" he asked.

We walked out of the hall, and I pointed to where she sat. I will never forget his words: "Which one? Is that your mother, in the dirty, rumpled kerchief?"

"Yes." Even in that crowd of exhausted and sad faces, my mother's frail and sickened condition singled her out. I told him that we were going to my brother, who lived near Polotsk.

He took me into the first-class waiting hall. Its cleanliness and order, in such contrast to the third-class waiting hall, astonished me. It held so few people! Fried chicken, sandwiches with caviar, and other food not available to most people were displayed under glass. People stood by the cashier's window. All the men and women were well dressed. Everyone's gaze immediately turned to us. They looked at me as if I were a monster—with dirty clothes, swollen legs in torn stockings, shabby galoshes, a dirty kerchief on my head, and a torn, wrinkled overcoat on my shoulders. I couldn't have made a pleasant impression on the elite.

The man approached an employee and spoke with him for a little while. He then approached the ticket window, paying absolutely no attention to the others, and began to talk with the cashier. I couldn't hear their conversation, but after several minutes he walked away from the window with two tickets in hand, went to the buffet, and asked the worker to make up a package of food. Together we made our way to the place where my mother was sitting.

She didn't know where I had gone; as I approached her accompanied by a stranger, bewilderment and fear crossed her face. The man extended the package to my mother. He explained that the train to Moscow would leave in forty-five minutes and that he would help us board it.

He took us out to the platform through the doors reserved for the privileged. People looked at us disapprovingly. Our patron went to the conductor of the car, said something to him, and then said good-bye to us, wishing us a good trip.

For a time we were alone in the compartment, and we savored the fried chicken and French rolls. Two young, well-groomed men in dark blue suits entered later. They sat down on the lower seats, because we had already occupied both upper berths.

The young men talked quietly between themselves. We couldn't figure out who these people were. Later, when they thought we were asleep, I noticed that one of them searched my mother, feeling through her clothing while she slept. Whether these men were connected to our patron or had happened into our compartment by chance was a mystery to us. After a while they vanished from our compartment.

I don't remember how many days we rode to Moscow, because in our exhaustion we tried to sleep most of the time. We knew we were nearing the capital only when the conductor announced our approach. What awaited us in Moscow?

The passengers quickly disembarked. We heard the delighted cries of relatives and friends meeting on the platform. Although there were people like us everywhere, even in Moscow, people still looked at us from every angle as we exited the car.

We went out onto the platform and merged with the flow of the crowd. I noticed a man in a railway uniform moving quickly toward us. He was examining everyone attentively. As soon as his gaze fell on us, he ran to us and said that he would take us to the Byelorusskii terminal. Again a mystery: How did he know of us? Why was he looking for us in particular? Who was he? Had the man in the gray suit informed him about us? He didn't ask our names or who we were. More important, we did not dare to ask who he was. We hopefully considered both strangers to be messengers from God. The man who met us even took a small package containing a pillow and a towel from my mother's hand and carried it for her.

He led us through the huge terminal. Exiting onto the street, we boarded a trolley and headed for the Byelorusskii terminal. From the window of the trolley I watched the streets of Moscow and the crowds of people moving like ants. When we arrived at the terminal, the stranger said that he would go to ask about the train schedule. He found out that the train for which we had tickets did not depart for a few hours, but that there was another which would leave in half an hour. For some reason he had to pay a difference in the tickets. There were no obstacles as he seated us in our places.

The question still nags at my mind: were both of these men sympathetic to those persecuted by Soviet power or did they simply have remorseful consciences, seeing what the authorities were doing to our people? I believe the first is more likely, although the question remains unanswered.

Since the train was going to Riga, near the Latvian border, we knew that they would check documents thoroughly, and we left the train in the city of Polotsk. We went on foot toward Baraukha, not suspecting that soldiers were concentrated in this region. It was dangerous, since the Soviets often detained people who had no documents. My mother and I passed through Baraukha unnoticed and spent the night with a poor peasant family. In the morning we again continued our journey. We walked along the highway, counting the distance by the posts set one hundred meters apart. We walked for several days, resting often.

We wanted to find my brother and his family, who lived near Borkovichi station, though we didn't know exactly where. We knew that Boris had been sent to this small town as a teacher, before our exile. He had worked as a teacher and school director in a rural region five hundred kilometers from our family's home. He and his wife had a small daughter, Erochka.

At last, we arrived at his village and discovered where they were living. It was the former home of a priest, which now housed three families: Boris, the secretary of the local trade union committee, and a widowed schoolteacher with her son. Walking up to this house, we saw curious faces watching us from windows. We looked terrible, so this was not surprising.

In all the time that had passed since we were sent to Siberia, we had known nothing about my brother and my sister's fate. We now learned that Marina was also living in this town. Our reunion was one of the greatest moments of my life. Everyone cried, except my brother's wife Zhenia and little Erochka, who looked at us in amazement, not understanding who these strange people were or what was happening. My brother's wife simply glared at us and exchanged an abrupt phrase with my brother.

My sister Marina prepared a bath, cut our hair, and burned our clothing in a bonfire. My feet and Mother's were covered with open wounds. The redness around the wounds was expanding. Marina ran to her friend, the doctor at the local hospital. She came and did everything necessary, and the next day we went to her office. She sent me to a dentist, since my teeth were loose and my gums were dark and bleeding. Rheumatism tormented me. Terrible shooting pains continued day and night in my legs and hands. I cried like a child from the pain. It was surprising that we had felt neither pain nor weakness when we were wandering through unknown places, but now, surrounded by the care of people close to us, we both felt unbearably sore.

Zhenia was obviously displeased and hardly spoke to us. She grumbled at my brother and nagged at him. One day I heard her exclaim, "I am not a slave to your relatives!" Boris looked at her, said nothing, and left the apartment. This added still more tension and sadness to our desperate situation. We had no place to go from here, even if we were able. Being on the road for more than a year had exhausted us to the limit, and neither of us thought we could bear further physical torment.

Although Boris was never on the list to be arrested, my sister had been on the list because of an incident at a May Day celebration. A drunken active Party member came up to Marina, said some disjointed flattering phrases to her, and began to propose marriage for his retarded son. When she turned to go away from him, he grabbed her breast. She turned and slapped his insolent face. All this happened quickly and in the presence of many witnesses.

"Well, we'll see! I'll show you, you . . ." he shouted oaths and other insulting words. "There won't be even ashes left of your parents' home. I will destroy all of you!"

The incident caused her name to be placed on a list of "enemies of the people." When she found out from relatives, Marina abandoned her studies and went into hiding for a long time. The authorities continued to search for her until she spread the rumor that she had gone insane. That foul drunkard calmed down when he heard that she had gone out of her mind, and the searches stopped.

After wandering among acquaintances and friends, Marina moved to my brother's home and, through my brother, got a job as a teacher in an elementary school.

My brother and sister tried as much as they could to be exceedingly attentive to us. Knowing that I had missed a lot of school, they both began to tutor me in various subjects. As a child, I had quickly memorized verses and fairy tales. Now I had to work on more serious subjects and, in spite of my physical indispositions, I succeeded in my studies. In the fall they enrolled me in the equivalent of eighth grade. I was fifteen. School came easily to me.

Just when it seemed as if life was going more normally, there was a loud knock on the door one rainy autumn night. My brother got up and opened the door. Representatives of the local authorities stood on the other side.

"Citizen Petrov?" said one of the uninvited visitors menacingly.

"Yes, I'm Petrov," answered my brother. "What's the matter?"

"You're under arrest," he answered.

"What for?" asked Boris, in confusion.

"For hiding your social origins."

"I don't understand you. What have I hidden?"

"Get ready and don't talk so much, it won't help you. Your parents are enemies of the people."

The whole family heard this conversation. Zhenia and Marina got out of bed and quietly watched. My mother and I lay silently, hardly breathing. We expected them to take us away as well. They took Boris away at about three o'clock in the morning. Five hours later, the representatives appeared again and announced that the family had to vacate the apartment by noon.

Zhenia decided to move to her mother's place, ten kilometers away from the village. Marina decided to go to the *oblast'* government to find out where our brother was being held and what needed to be done to get him out of prison.

In spite of the unnerving situation, I went to school that morning. When I entered the long corridor, my classmates pointed at me and cried, "Enemy of the people! Enemy of the people!" These were the same students who had earlier fawned on me when they had discovered that I was the director's sister. Now I had suddenly become an "enemy of the people."

When I returned from school in tears, my brother's family's furniture and belongings, thrown outdoors, had already become soggy in the rain. The keys to the apartment had been turned over to some active Party member. My sister-in-law sat with Erochka beneath a tree and waited for Marina, hoping that she could obtain a cart to load the things and go to her mother's. My mother sat under another tree, absorbed in deep thought. She decided to stay with her own relatives, even though parents often were repudiated by their children. Neither relatives nor close friends, in fear for their own fate, would extend a helping hand during those days of terror.

I don't know how Marina obtained a horse, harnessed to a long four-wheeled cart. She jumped down and we began to load the things.

"Marinochka, take me to the station, I'm going to Semeon's," requested my mother (Semeon was my mother's brother). My sister became thoughtful and looked at her quietly.

"Wait for me, I'll be right back," answered Marina. She ran toward the hospital. Although we at first didn't know why, when she returned it became clear that she had gone to borrow money from her friend the doctor to give to Mother for the trip.

We went to Zhenia's mother's place first. It was late evening when we reached the village. She lived with her younger daughter in a small hut that looked like it was on spindly legs. They were already both asleep when we drove up to their hut, and they knew nothing about what had happened.

Zhenia's father had been a Red partisan who had been killed in a skirmish with the White Army during the Civil War.[9] Her mother eked out a pitiful existence and had become very tyrannical. She unmercifully beat her younger daughter and sometimes also attacked Zhenia. Because she had refused to enter the *kolkhoz*, her land was taken from her. All she had was a tiny farm, a horse, a cow, and some pigs. Her livestock were not allowed to graze on the collective farm's land.

My sister-in-law went into the hut and, after a lengthy conversation, came out with her younger sister to unload the things. Almost everything was placed in the barn, since there was no room in the hut. We went into the hut fearfully and made ourselves comfortable on the floor. I fell asleep, but Mother and Marina never closed their eyes.

Early the next day we got up and set off for the station. Sick at heart, we put Mother on the train. It began to move, and a feeling came over me as if something had been torn from my body. I wanted to go with her. I couldn't believe that the time had come to part from my mother, perhaps forever. Where was she going? What awaited her? It was impossible to foresee the circumstances that shaped our future. First my father had left for points unknown, and now my mother was going away. I felt truly alone and wept silently. Marina began to cry. That proud beauty had always been an example of stoicism, but now she also felt helpless before the destructive, merciless elements.

Marina had to return to her work at the school, heavy with the fear that she also would be arrested. I remained with my sister-in-law and gradually recovered from the rigors of the past months. As soon as I was able, I enrolled at the school where Zinaida, Zhenia's sister, studied. The school was five kilometers from the hut, so I had to get up early.

The third day after our arrival, Zhenia's mother woke me at three in the morning and ordered me to take the horse into the woods to the pasture. She gave me directions and added that I had to return in time so as not to be late for school. I was still very weak, but I couldn't object, because I feared this witch. The horse was thin, resembling its worn-out owner. I had known how to ride since early childhood, but not on such sick horses. My frail body against the horse's hard bones did not bring back memories of the pleasant horseback rides of my youth.

Since I was left alone among strangers, I was becoming more and more silent. I remembered reading once about the life of the writer Maxim Gorky, who had lived among strangers from the age of seven. They had all jeered at him for being an orphan. The Soviet government criticized pre-revolutionary life, but what of the "happy" life now? "Thank you, Soviet powers, for all the humiliations," I thought bitterly while riding to the woods.

I walked to school each day with Zinaida. She was not very bright, learned slowly, and had remained for two years at almost every grade level. Although I had missed several years, I was a year ahead of her and helped her with lessons. She and her mother tried to create obstacles to my education. For example, I could not read in the evening because I was not allowed to burn the kerosene. Nevertheless, I bore everything patiently and tried to fit in without tears. I resolved to absorb everything to receive an education. I had bags under my eyes from lack of sleep and bad nourishment.

One time Marina came to visit and was frightened by my appearance. She had continued working at the school, but they warned her that she would lose her job at the end of the quarter. A Party worker told her that "people like her" were not allowed to work in the border region. She quickly moved and found a job in an elementary school not far from the city of Vitebsk. She later became head of that school.

Because of the distance, it was difficult for her to petition the authorities to free Boris from prison. Her beauty and sharp mind defeated her enemies, however, and Boris was released from prison. Because of the acute shortage of mathematics teachers, my brother was sent to teach in a remote *oblast'* with no questions asked. A month later he came for his family. I was boundlessly happy to see him, my beloved brother and my defender. Our meeting was darkened, however, by the fact that on that same evening my sister-in-law's mother attacked her with a pitchfork. If my brother hadn't intervened, she probably would have been seriously wounded.

Boris was attentive to me. He began to ask how I felt, living here without relatives. I didn't have time to say even a word when his wife began to yell at both of us. "We have suffered because of your relatives, you were in prison because of them, and now you are interested in her life, but not mine!" she screamed.

"You live with your mother, and it's not my fault she's crazy," he retorted irritably. "This is my sister, and she's suffered enough. I will not abandon my mother and sisters, and I will never renounce them." He continued, "Marina tore me from the talons of the NKVD, but what did you do?"

I cried, holding my little niece closely. She had loved me from our first meeting and always sought my defense when her mother beat her unmercifully for any little thing. Zhenia's despotism obviously had been inherited from her mother. Zhenia was uneducated and had lived with her aunt in Moscow for some time. She had evidently run away to her aunt's after her mother's beatings.

I often remembered how our mother grieved, knowing whom Boris had married. She had immediately sensed the different temperaments of the two newlyweds. Boris met his future wife, who was a few years older, when he was sent far from home as a young, inexperienced teacher. He had to get married because Zhenia was already four months pregnant. After the marriage, he stopped writing home, not wanting to acknowledge his mistake.

Alarmed by her son's sudden silence, Mother insisted that Father go search for him and find out why he hadn't returned home in time for vacation. Her anxiety was so great that she even fell ill. Father found his son and, to his great surprise, a daughter-in-law and granddaughter named Valeriia (Erochka). He sent a telegram home that everything was all right, that Boris was alive. The three of them were living with Zhenia's mother. Soon after this, we were banished to Siberia, and no one except Father had ever met the in-laws.

The closeness of our family annoyed my sister-in-law and her mother endlessly. Nobody experienced the cruelty of these savage people as much as I, who seemed to have fallen from the flames of one fire into another. Although I was always sad and pensive, I never complained to my brother about my treatment. I dreamed of completing my education and establishing my future.

To my brother's questions of who was hurting me, I always responded: nobody. I knew that he understood the situation. He once tried to comfort me by saying, "Don't grieve, little sister; on this earth, happiness, like unhappiness, is not eternal. Happiness, like the rays of the sun, emerges and again goes behind a cloud." These words have echoed in my ears all of my life.

The exceptional attention he lavished on me made his wife jealous and further complicated my life in his absence. Zhenia made me do all the housework. I often thought that I was like Cinderella but never harbored thoughts that a prince would save me. I used any free moment to read or fulfill school assignments.

When Boris was transferred to another school, Marina took me in. She had obtained an apartment at the school, with another teacher. Marina then began to search for Mother. After several months, one of our relatives let us know of our mother's whereabouts, and my sister immediately sent her money for a ticket. Mother arrived shortly thereafter.

I went to the secondary school about five kilometers away. It was a new school and needed teachers. Since we understood from my brother's letters that his home life was not entirely pleasant, Marina helped him get a job there. Boris moved with his family into my sister's apartment. It was crowded, since there were only two bedrooms and seven people in the apartment. But by the standards of life in our country, this was luxurious.

In late autumn, Zhenia decided she wanted to go to Moscow to visit her aunt. We were all pleased at the idea and were glad to live without her shouts and animosity, if only for a short time.

My brother and I walked to school each morning and returned home toward five o'clock. In the evenings we all gathered in one room, talking and laughing. We were busy with our own business and we all finished our own tasks. Boris was at his peak as a teacher and as a person. Students and teachers alike respected him for his sensitivity and courtesy.

Time passed quickly, and after several months our situation changed again when my brother's family returned from Moscow. My little niece Erochka was glad to see all of us and called me Aunt Lenochka. I always spent much time with her, trundled her about on a sled, and comforted her when she cried after beatings. Because he was so busy, Boris did not know about all our problems. Moreover, our mother was seriously ill and lay in bed all the time. Marina and I looked after her.

Before the move to the elementary school, Marina had already gotten to know a very handsome chemistry teacher, Peter Il'ich. None of our family liked him. He was a product of Soviet upbringing, very proud and devoted to his Young Communist League ideals. Love is blind, however, and after a year Marina announced to us that she was thinking of getting married. Boris had to think of finding a new place to work and an apartment for his family. We could not remain in my sister's apartment since she was to move in with her husband and be replaced by a new teacher.

Boris began to search for a new place of work nearer a cultural center, where he could indulge his taste for the theater. He received a favorable recommendation from the school, and we moved to a small city ninety kilometers from the city of Vitebsk. The director of the school was a historian named Levitskii, who had graduated from the University of Kazan. His wife, Valentina Ivanovna, was a cultured woman who taught zoology. They gave my brother an apartment, next to the school, with a large room with a kitchen. Taking into account the state in which teachers lived, the arrangement was excellent. The only negative aspect was that I was again under the full control of my sister-in-law. My brother was busy with his work at school, so I was always with her.

My legs still troubled me, especially in changes of weather, when they hurt unbearably. The swelling gradually diminished, but my walk was not dainty. When she saw how I walked, Mother would look at me with grief. All our family feared that I would remain crippled all my life.

Later, my mother's brother, a doctor and professor of medicine, helped me immeasurably by trying to restore my nerves and prescribing medication. He probably saved me from being permanently disabled.

Like so many others, this man had suffered too, but he was able to establish a reputation as a medical specialist by hiding his connections with the past. He used his mother's maiden name and managed to get his medical degree in Moscow. He helped many with fates similar to ours—not only spiritually, but materially. His most important contribution to me, however, was his insistence that I chart a new course for my life, that I believe in myself and search for my own happiness.

My uncle's help, my determination to survive all hardships and be a physically normal person, and my youth were all elements that aided my recovery. Despite my ailments, my mind was strong. In classes, I listened attentively and, after a good explanation by the teacher, I absorbed and mastered the material without difficulty.

My brother often worked with me when he had time. Besides his favorite subjects—mathematics and physics—he loved to read and knew all the leading figures in world literature. Books held the greatest value for him. His wide-ranging interests inspired me as well.

"Remember, Lena," he would tell me often, "a book is a source of knowledge, and no one can take away acquired knowledge. The authorities can take away everything except your own thoughts."

My parents told me that when I was young I used to gather children of my own age and, stamping my foot, "instruct" them in reading and writing. I did consider other occupations briefly. When I completed secondary school, I informed my brother that I wanted to enroll in a medical institute.

"No, my dear! That's not for you," Boris said. "With your sensitive attitude toward every sufferer, if your first patient died, you would die along with him." This was true, since I couldn't bear the sight of blood. "You begin to cry when you see the tears of others," he continued. "And you want to be a doctor? No, instead go by the road that fate and your talent point out to you!"

Taking his advice, I yielded and enrolled in a pedagogical institute. I never regretted this later in life, and to this day I love my profession. I love young people, and I always feel an unbelievable joy in seeing the pupils' progress. I believe that it is a great privilege, a gift from God, to share my knowledge with the rising generation. I remember all the poverty of student life, but those were the greatest years. No poverty can stop the flight of thoughts that somewhere ahead awaits a happier future; it helps one to endure any difficulties.

Chapter Two

A Ray of Happiness

1

When I arrived at the Pedagogical Institute in Vitebsk in the fall of 1935, I did not have a place to stay because there were not enough places in the student dormitory. I became depressed and sat in a corridor with a group of new female students. Many of them were in the same situation and had to find at least a corner to call home. One girl, named Roza Goldman, came up and joined in the general conversation. She was pleasant to everyone. When she learned that I didn't have a room to live in, she immediately suggested that I go to her parents' home, hoping that perhaps they would help me. The Goldmans were a loving Jewish family. Although poor, they had their own small house. The father worked in a factory, and the mother was a dressmaker, which explained why Roza was so well dressed. Of the three children (two daughters and a younger son) Roza was the eldest.

I lived with them for an entire year, until I was assigned a place in the dormitory. Many times I didn't have even a kopek, but these kind people shared everything they had with me. I slept in Roza's room on a small bed with a straw mattress. I didn't have any possessions of my own except for a few poor clothes. Food was very sparse. Although I received a monthly stipend for good academic progress, I could never make it through the month.

I spent most of my free time in the library. The institute often had student parties and dances, but I did not participate. Even though I would have liked to enjoy an active social life, I didn't have any clothes or shoes appropriate for going out. Most important, I feared that the people at the institute would expel me if they discovered my past: my exile in Siberia, my escape, and my claim to be an orphan, when in fact my mother and perhaps even my father were still alive, weighed heavily upon me. Claiming to be an orphan spared me unnecessary explanations and problems, especially having to produce required documents about my social origin. Being an orphan simply made it easier to exist.

Although I was all skin and bones and frequently had swollen knees and ankles, my girlfriends told me that I was lovely, which gave me confidence. Although the expression on my face was always sad, my heart was filled with joy for the chance to study and be a part of a circle of people my own age. Some boys noticed me, and several wrote love letters. I didn't answer any of them since I directed all of my energy to my studies.

The worst times of my student life were vacations, because I had nowhere to go. Boris was always glad to see me, but Zhenia disliked me terribly. Marina was married, had two children, and lived far away with our invalid mother, who was hiding from the authorities. Without documents or passport, my mother could not be registered to live in that area. The passport was of the utmost importance for registration, but as a fugitive from Siberia she could not get one. I didn't know where my father was or whether he was still alive.

Peter, my sister's husband, was a great fanatic and admirer of the regime, but he loved his wife and his charming children. Their elder boy, Boris, was almost three and the little girl, Lorisa, was nine months old. At the time, both of them closely resembled my sister. I adored both my niece and nephew.

I once went to their place for a few days and witnessed an unpleasant exchange between Peter and Marina concerning our family. "They deserved it and they were banished," Peter uttered with malice.

My sister was at this time serving dinner. She threw a full bowl of borshch on the table. "My family had done nothing to your authorities!" she shouted in anger.

He got up, wiped borshch from his clothing, put on

his cap, and stalked outside. Mother and I had kept silent until that moment, but as soon as he left we both attacked Marina.

"Marina, have you lost your mind? Is it really necessary to act so? After all, he is your husband!" said my mother tearfully.

"And you are my mother, and I wouldn't part with you for anyone! Let's not allow him to defend so strongly the justice of those who have power!" exclaimed Marina.

All three of us cried.

After a short period, Peter returned, apologized to her, and, approaching my mother, kissed her hand (which had never happened before) and apologized to her. "You understand me," he said in measured tones. "I must hold to my line, otherwise we will all be back in Siberia. I don't want my children to take the path that your daughter Lena has experienced."

He turned toward me. "In my eyes, Lena, you are a real heroine. I've never said this, but now, when I've insulted my wife and all of you, your suffering flashes before my eyes. I am guilty, so please forgive me! We are powerless to change everything that happens around us."

We all listened to him silently and with full comprehension. Finally, Mother broke the silence: "For me it is especially difficult. I'm sick, a complete invalid, and I have nowhere to go. I don't want to be a burden to you, but where can I go? Why hasn't the Lord taken me, when I have already been on the edge of death several times?" Looking at me, she asked, "Why did you save me from death, Lena?"

Marina and I approached her, hugged her, and cried aloud with her. "Be there prison, be there exile, I will not abandon my mother," Marina declared to her husband. "I will not throw her out to be eaten by bloodthirsty wolves!"

From this time on, my sister's husband became more friendly to us.

We understood Peter's fears. If the bureaucrats learned that Mother was living there without a passport and consequently without permission to be in this region, they would immediately arrest Peter, expel him from the Party, and deprive him of the right to be a teacher. We grasped the entire situation and knew it was impossible to find a way out of it.

My heart ached, but the sheer force of my sister's will gave me strength and inspired me to hope and plan for a better future. On the other hand, hope was a rare commodity. What was there to hope for? People were intimidated and embittered. Their only thoughts, painted against a backdrop of fear, focused on where to stand in line to obtain a kilogram of bread to feed the family.

I often contemplated how our people could endure all this fear and deprivation. Students in any country experience some shortages, but the way we lived meant we often went to sleep hungry and were glad for a piece of black bread and hot water tinged with the horrible smell of chlorine. At lectures in the auditorium, it was difficult to concentrate. My head swam and colored spots spun before my eyes, all caused by incessant hunger. No one dared to complain about the shortages, although we all understood each other's plight.

When I was in the third year of the institute, our family received information from relatives that Father was alive, living in Leningrad and working in an automobile repair plant. A decent person had helped him to get a job and to hide the traces of his past by changing his surname. This news gave me an unbelievable desire to see my father again. He eventually learned through other people where the rest of the family and I lived.

How I yearned to live together again with both my parents as before—but we all knew this was impossible. Times had changed, and we had changed in the intervening years. In order to survive, my father was hiding his past. My mother was a completely helpless invalid.

Returning to the dormitory after a lecture one day, I found a summons to the telephone station for the next evening at six o'clock. This frightened me very much, since no one had ever called me on the telephone. Only the very privileged had telephones at home, of course, and common people could not dream of such a luxury. In order to speak by telephone, one had to go to the telephone station and place a request, indicating to whom you wanted to speak and the time and place of the call. It was also expensive. Now someone was calling me. Who could this be? That was a sleepless night followed by a long day. I reported to the telephone station fifteen minutes early and gave the operator the summons. Twenty minutes later, my name was called, and I learned the number of the booth where I could receive my call.

My heart began to race when I heard my father's voice over the wire.

"My dear little daughter!" exclaimed my father.

I couldn't utter a word and burst into tears. Knowing that these moments cost money, I said in a trembling voice, "Is it really you, Papa?"

He wanted to know all about me—my health, my studies, my difficulties. We skipped from one subject to another. Our conversation was too short, and we didn't even have time to say good-bye, because they cut us off.

When I returned to the dormitory, my friends gathered around me with questions: "Who called you?" Sadly, I couldn't tell them that it was my father, because they all thought I was an orphan. I had to free myself from this web and tell a lie. I claimed that the call was from a lieutenant friend whom I happened to have met on the train.

"Oh, then that means he's taken an interest in you!" said the girls in chorus.

"Yes, apparently!" I answered, embarrassed.

"What is he like?" my good friend Anya asked me.

"Very handsome and intelligent," I answered. "He is a serious fellow, and I like him." This was not a complete deception, for there was a lieutenant who was attracted to me. Arkadii Lomonosov was a direct descendant of Mikhail Lomonosov himself.[1] In contrast to many soldiers, he was well read. I liked talking with him. Arkadii wrote me long letters and came to see me whenever he could. Thus, I found a way out of the predicament.

My beloved father's voice echoed in my ears for a long time after the telephone call. "I am not alone," I thought to myself. "I have a father, he is alive and even working!" But my joy was periodically replaced by fear. "What if they find out about Father!" After all, at the auto repair plant authorities investigated the workers well before they were allowed to work. Nevertheless, I cherished the hope of seeing him. Afterward, on very rare occasions, my father called me. We eventually made arrangements to meet in Leningrad sometime in the future.

I began to go out in the evening with other young people. I loved to attend the theaters and cinema and took advantage of free tickets whenever possible. As always, my horribly poor appearance embarrassed me.

My roommate at the dormitory was a beautiful and good-hearted girl named Anya. Her parents lived and worked on a collective farm. They were poor but always told Anya to bring me home with her on the holidays. Visiting them, I saw how peasants suffered. How hard it was for them to work and live with such terrible shortages! Small plots of land (fifteen hundredths of a hectare) were adjacent to the homes of the collective farmers. They could work on these plots only after their workday on the collective farm.

Anya had a friend, a mathematics teacher named Evgenii, whom she liked very much. I was not so sure of his feelings toward her, although I didn't tell her of my suspicions. He did not see her often.

One beautiful day in late May, I went to the post office to mail a letter to my father. It was a considerable distance, so I was gone for a long while. Meanwhile, Evgenii came to see us at the dormitory with his friend Anton, also a mathematics teacher. They invited us to a picnic in the country. They had studied together at the university and had become inseparable friends. Besides their studies together, their origins also bound them together; they were both descended from the Polish Catholic gentry.

Since I wasn't home, the three of them left without me. Later, Anya told me that Anton was very disappointed: he very much wanted to meet me, after seeing my photograph on the nightstand.

In June the school year ended, and for me the sad times came again. Where should I go? While both Marina and Boris extended invitations, either option had disadvantages. Marina lived far away and my sister-in-law didn't like me or my family. She was jealous of our education since she had only a smattering. Zhenia could not resign herself to the fact that her sister, a poor student, was stuck in the sixth year of school. I pitied Zinaida and quietly blamed her misfortunes on her cruel and half-crazy mother, who continually mocked and beat her. The bruises on her face and body never had a chance to heal before her mother hit her again. What kind of learning could there be when she experienced this kind of life?

Nevertheless, I decided to go to my brother's home for the summer. There were four apartments in the house where my brother and his family lived. Teachers from the secondary school lived in them. In front of the house was a large fruit orchard, and next to it were the tenants' little gardens. A small, deep river flowed beyond the orchard. There were all kinds of fish in it, and I enjoyed swimming in its cool, clear water.

In the summer, secondary school pupils and university students vacationing in the country gathered on the banks. Weeping willows with many birds' nests drooped over the river, and the sloping riverside meadows seemed like a green carpet. Nightingales evoked delight and love with their singing. We all got to know each other, made dates, and listened to the evening songs of the birds. The time passed beautifully and romantically.

One day while swimming in the river, I nearly drowned when a strong current dragged me into a whirlpool. I began to scream, since I swam poorly and feared the water. Fortunately, there were many excellent swimmers nearby. One of them was a student at the Polytechnic Institute named Sergei Sidorov. He quickly swam to me, grabbed me around the waist with his strong arms, and pulled me to a safe shallow place. The next day, when I went to take a swim, my friends sang to me a couplet they had composed:

> But Sidorov, the rascal,
> Drags Lena out of the whirlpool;
> Having lowered Lena there,
> He swims away to catch another . . .

Sergei and I became great friends, and some girls regarded our relationship jealously. It was fun to be with him, because we could talk about anything. He was always cheerful. His tactful behavior reflected the influence of a good family. He was tall, lean, athletic, and always neatly dressed. His father was the station master at a railroad terminal. Sergei was the youngest in the family. His sisters, living in Moscow, were well educated and lived with their husbands, who had good jobs. Occasionally, they came to visit their parents.

This little town had several very cultured families. Their grown children studied at higher educational institutions but came home during summer vacation. In this way, they cultivated a circle of old friends each year. I was welcomed into this circle of young people. We all shared a common interest in literature, music, and theater. We organized nature hikes, picnics, read poetry, and gave orations.

There were two sisters, very nice girls, in our group. They were the daughters of Dr. Pirozhkov. One had just finished secondary school, and the second was in the ninth year. They had a wonderful home. Since Dr. Pirozhkov worked in Moscow and his wife stayed with him, a maid lived with the girls in place of their parents. It surprised me that Dr. Pirozhkov and his wife very rarely visited their own children, and I wondered why they all didn't move to Moscow. Ira, the older daughter, had a crush on Sergei, who was warmer to me than to her. When we all got together, he was usually at my side.

My summer with Boris passed happily until I received a letter from my sister. She asked me to come visit for two weeks. I set off, although I didn't want to part from my friends, especially Sergei.

My sister met me at the station. I was glad to see her, but I understood from the abrupt conversation that our mother was very ill and the doctor feared for her life. I couldn't wait to see her. When we entered the apartment, she tried to get up, but could not. I ran to her bed and, hiding my tears, embraced and kissed her. In contrast to her younger days, she was now a thin, pale old woman. Of her once-beautiful curly hair only very scanty gray wisps remained. Her cheerless but expressive eyes reflected without words that feeling which is known only to mothers at the sight of their children.

"Lenusenka, my dear little daughter, how happy I am

to see you," she whispered. "Come sit by me. I thought that I would die and not see you before my death."

"No, Mamusenka," I answered. "I came to spend two weeks with you—you will get better."

Her heart was failing. There were irregularities in her heartbeat, and it was hard for her to breathe. My arrival cheered her, and she slowly began to raise herself a little and to sit up for short periods. She looked me over closely from head to toe and expressed satisfaction that my legs had become more normal. She asked me to tell her all about my life, my studies, and my friends. She asked if I were in love with anyone. My sister and I had always shared our lives with her, so I slowly tried to tell her everything, not hiding any detail.

I told her about my first love. While I was still in secondary school, a tenth-year student named Vladimir sent me my first love letter. He asked me to meet him by the pump house. After I declined, he followed me as I walked to the store for some bread and offered to take me for a ride on his bicycle. In those days it was a big deal to have a bicycle. He told his mother about me, and she was very friendly when we met. One day she even invited me to their home. I could tell she was a good housewife because the house was very clean and cozy.

An accomplished pianist, Vladimir's mother played several pieces by Tchaikovsky, my favorite composer. Vladimir's face shone with happiness that I was comfortable with his mother. Likewise, his parents adored him. He also played the piano. He was studious and, influenced by his father, enrolled in the Polytechnic Institute. His departure marked the end of my first love.

Another experience I told Mother about happened during my last year of secondary school and first year at the Pedagogical Institute. There was a young poet and teacher of Byelorussian literature named Leonid Ivanov who came to our school. He became very good friends with my brother, who was at this time the academic vice-president of the school. Leonid often dropped by our place and dined with us occasionally. We all went together to the cinema or to concerts at the factory clubs.

Our dates became frequent. During one of our meetings, on the bank of the river, he declared his love for me. My brother approved of our relationship. We wrote to each other, and he often came to the city to spend his free day with me.

Distance either can create an incredible longing between two people or can act to cool feelings. Although the opportunities existed, I avoided many social activities to remain true to Leonid and not to interrupt my studies. While I was loyal, however, a female doctor began to chase after Leonid. At first I didn't know this, but I learned about it from my girlfriends when I visited Boris during winter vacation. Leonid swore that he loved only me. The vacation ended, and we parted as before. When we saw each other again the following June, he was very ill with a fever. He had begun to drink terribly during our separation, explaining this as a result of his yearning for me. (I have never liked heavy drinkers.) He proposed marriage and invited me to accompany him to his parents' home in the country.

I considered his proposal but decided to put an end to this love affair. He left for his parents' home alone and ailing. A month passed without a letter from him. Finally he wrote that upon arriving home he had become still worse. After a few days, he felt better and decided to write. I remember several lines from the letter even to this day:

> And my thoughts fly into the distance; don't look upon me, roses in the small window, don't cause sadness to my soul. I am in love and am abandoned to suffering, fate has severed her from me. The image is subjected only to memory, never again to find one so dear.

A crack had appeared in our relationship, however; I had no feelings left for him except pity. When he returned in autumn, I was already gone. Our correspondence continued, but our meetings became rarer. During the winter vacation, I dropped by my brother's for a few days. While waiting for the train, I watched Leonid as he walked around the terminal several times. He was hurt and unbelievably angry. We silently parted forever.

Mother listened attentively to my stories and only advised me to approach the question of love seriously. "For everything there is a destiny," she advised solemnly.

The two weeks flew by quickly. I had to return to the institute via my brother's to collect my few possessions. Upon arrival I learned that Dr. Pirozhkov's daughter Irina had become very intimate with Sergei. A little later it became known that she was pregnant. They sent for her father and mother from Moscow, and the parents from both sides concluded that Sergei must marry Irina. No sooner said than done.

In the following months, when I went to my brother's on vacations, Sergei and I occasionally ran into each other at the cinema or at a concert. Our gazes met quietly and we exchanged many unspoken thoughts, but such was the fate of our love. Soon after their child was born, Sergei's father was arrested and sentenced to ten years' imprisonment for having a negligent attitude toward work. A log had fallen from a loaded flatcar and caused a passenger train to wreck. Sergei also was condemned for this, for I later heard that he was expelled from the institute. I never learned of their subsequent fate.

2

I continued with my studies at the institute, all the time eagerly awaiting my reunion with Father in Leningrad in December 1937. Before my trip, I caught a bad cold and completely lost my voice. Because I didn't want to postpone the long-awaited reunion, I wouldn't listen to advice that I postpone the journey. No one could stop me, not even my dear brother, whose counsel I always welcomed and usually took.

On the way to Leningrad, I sent my father a telegram so that he would meet me at the terminal. The journey took more than a day. Finally the train arrived, and the city of Leningrad cheerlessly greeted passengers to its cold winter and bone-chilling wind. I hadn't been able to buy a gift for my father, but I had bought several pounds of tart winter apples for him from a woman from a collective farm. She had somehow managed to keep them until the middle of winter. What a tasty, aromatic treat these apples were! My big suitcase was filled with apples instead of clothing. It was hard to carry.

The passengers streamed onto the platform and headed for the terminal. I walked slowly, for I had little strength to carry the heavy suitcase. Friends or relatives met many of the passengers. I stopped and searched the crowd for my father and saw no one who looked like him.

He must not have received my telegram, I thought to myself. I knew from prior conversations that the First Automobile Repair Plant where he worked was somewhere in the direction of Sredniaia Rogatka.[2] At the information bureau I found out that one of two trolleys would take me to the plant. I headed toward the stop with my baggage. A man and a woman were standing at the stop. I remember that the woman was wearing a fur jacket, and the man was in a dark-blue uniform, though not a military one.

I approached the woman to make sure that I would be able to catch the correct trolley at this stop. She couldn't even answer my question before someone seized me by the shoulders from behind and cried, "Lenok, my dear daughter!"

The man standing there with tears in his eyes and wearing the strange uniform turned out to be my father. He had been at the terminal but had not recognized his own daughter, and I had not recognized him. Only when he heard my hoarse voice did he intuitively realize who I was.

Indeed, many years had passed since we had parted in Siberia. He and I had looked horrible then, with faces twisted by disease and grief. Now a physically attractive man stood before me, and the uniform gave him a completely different appearance. In turn, he was not looking at a little girl clothed in dirty rags, covered by scabs and sores, hobbling on swollen legs. He was greeting a tall, slender young woman in a hat and a poor but clean overcoat.

The bitter wind pierced through my thin coat and chilled my entire body. I shivered both from the cold and from joy.

"My dear Papochka, I am happy to see you alive, that you have recovered. Is this a dream? It is you, it is you, my own flesh and blood!" I hugged him and kissed his cheeks. Frost had formed on his mustache.

The trolley approached, and we got on, riding a long time before reaching the plant. My father lived in a dormitory with many men, although I don't remember now how many lived in the large room. I slept in my father's bed the first night, since he was on the night watch at the plant as a guard. The next day he introduced me to several women from the women's dormitory, and they invited me to stay with them. Their dormitory was more comfortable, with a large communal kitchen. The rooms were clean and each had four to six beds, in contrast to the twenty-five or more beds in the men's section.

One kind lady from Yaroslavl, Anna Yakovlevna, treated me just like a daughter. My cold had worsened on the trip to Leningrad, and I developed a fever and a cough. Where earlier I had only talked hoarsely, now I completely lost my voice. Anna Yakovlevna took charge of my care.

The majority of the female workers at the plant were illiterate peasants. Several of them crossed themselves while lying in bed, so that no one would notice in the darkness. Seeing this, I thought to myself that it is not possible to kill the deep religious belief that has become rooted in our people throughout the centuries. No matter how the godless authorities of the Soviet Union tried, it would not be possible to expel faith in God from the hearts of the Russian people. The peasants were and continue to be the foundation of our Orthodox tradition. Without unnecessary questions, analyses, or criticisms, they preserve that deep faith, which they guard like a small spark in their hearts.

Anna Yakovlevna kept me in bed for several days. Orthodox Christmas Eve approached. After work that evening, all of the female workers dressed up and were quietly talking among themselves. At first I was uncomfortable and thought they were saying something about me, perhaps because I was disturbing them here. I was mistaken. Anna Yakovlevna came up to me and asked, almost in a whisper,

"Lena, would you like to go with us to church? Today is Christmas Eve; tomorrow is our Orthodox Christmas."

At these words my heart started to pound. Yes, I very much wanted to go with them. I was glad to be assured that not all religion had died in the hearts of these simple but wonderful people. I knew that faith in God had given me strength and patience to endure all difficulties, to struggle with fear, and to emerge as the victor over death. How many times had death visited my door? How many times in my struggle for life had I slammed my door shut when death knocked?

Yet now, when they suggested that I go with them to pray in a small chapel in a cemetery where an old priest, spared from execution and exile and not fearing anyone, celebrated the ritual of our Orthodoxy in secret, I was frightened. "No, I cannot go," I told Anna Yakovlevna.

Everyone in the group stared at me. There was neither contempt nor hatred in their eyes, but understanding of what a visit to a church could mean: expulsion from the institute. Fear stopped me. My faith was strong, but when the question was of life or death, weakness and self-doubt set in.

My father noticed that I had almost no decent clothing, and we decided to go with Anna Yakovlevna to purchase material. We went to a dry-goods store one evening and waited in line at the door for the entire night. When the store opened the next morning, Father bought ten meters of cambric, and Anna Yakovlevna bought three meters of green velvet. From the cambric we sewed undergarments and from the velvet, a dress.

"You also need shoes," Father observed. He went into town and brought back a pair of dark brown shoes. My appearance was immediately transformed.

Father took me with him to the plant dining hall, where Andreev, the plant *politruk*,[3] approached us. Father introduced me to him. I could sense a cultured upbringing in this man, in contrast to many *politruki*. After a short conversation, he offered my father tickets to the Kirovskii Theater.

"You must show your daughter the charms of Leningrad," said Andreev. I was delighted by this offer since the theater was my weakness. There were times at the institute when I only had enough money in my pocket for either a theater ticket or a modest meal, and I always chose the theater. Now, with free tickets to the Kirovskii Theater, I was ecstatic.

That evening Father and I set off for the theater. Since my dress and shoes were new, I decided not to wear my old galoshes, but the wind and frost were unbearable. In line I hid my feet beneath my overcoat, standing on one leg, holding onto Father. I will never forget how I suffered in the cold that evening from my own foolishness, and thoughts of my time in Siberia floated through my mind. There had been no alternative there, but here at the theater it was vanity. I was very glad when we entered.

I was struck by the theater's beauty and luxurious appearance. My heart soared. I scrutinized everything, including the well-dressed audience comprised of the Soviet elite and many officers. It goes without saying that there were very few simple people, such as my father and me, at the theater.

Our seats were in the twelfth row of the orchestra. People looked at us curiously when we took our seats, perhaps because of our modest attire or our differing ages. In appearance I was a copy of Father. He had completely changed from the time in Siberia when Mother had bid him a sad farewell. Now he looked young and smart with his gray-green eyes, straight, handsome nose, light-reddish mustache, and fair hair. His smile was beautiful.

There was still an empty seat next to me. Just before the opening of the curtain, Andreev himself sat down hastily, greeting us politely. I was a bit confused by this surprise. Father had told me earlier that Andreev was married and that he had two children. I asked myself: why is he alone? Evidently he had his own philosophy with regard to family life. The production was excellent, and the actors were flawless. The next day Andreev invited me to go to the Hermitage, which had been the winter palace of the tsar. After the 1917 Revolution, it had been transformed into a famous art museum. Although not all the rooms were open, I wandered around and admired the art of this remarkable museum the whole day.

To me this all seemed like a fairy tale or a deep sleep. The art and culture of Leningrad were such contrasts to Siberia and the prison camp. Could I reconcile this contrast in my mind? Leningrad was the pride of our Russian history, and the wonders of the Hermitage did not belong to the so-called builders of a new life, who destroyed the historic monuments of our culture assembled over the course of a thousand years. Peter's city was created by the torments of our laboring people. I was almost sorry that I had come here in the winter; how beautiful it would be here in spring or summer.

The day with Andreev passed delightfully, and I returned to the dormitory quite late. Anna Yakovlevna, who learned from my father where I had gone that day, waited up to eat supper with me. I worried, however, that because I was with Andreev something unpleasant would happen. After all, he was a married man. Nevertheless, he conducted himself very tactfully. We talked about art and the city. Andreev was born in Leningrad. He grew up, studied, and now worked here. His love for the city could be felt in his descriptions of the places we visited.

At the end of my stay he asked me if I would like to transfer to the Leningrad Institute. My answer was that I would, but that I preferred to finish where I already had a foundation. The teachers at my institute treated me well, I had a circle of my own friends, and I was close to my brother and sister. These factors weighed heavily against my coming to Leningrad. Most important, I again feared identification as a fugitive from Siberia, which would ruin my father's established life.

As I later understood, my dear father enjoyed great success with women. One day, quite surprisingly, he appealed to me with an unusual request. "Lenok," he began quietly, "do me a great favor. Don't tell anyone that Mama is still alive. As you can see, these women are after me. Indeed, I have already lived alone for so long, I have to do laundry and cook, and they have a mind to do me a favor."

My poor mother, regardless of her invalid state, often thought about him. With pain she would wonder, "How is my dear Georgii? I pray for his health. Who knows, perhaps he is no longer among the living and we must pray for his

soul." When we learned that he was alive, that he had re-
covered and was working, her face reflected a peaceful joy.
She crossed herself and quietly said, "I give thanks to you,
Lord!"

When he made this request, I looked at my father with
wide-eyed astonishment. I knew how he had loved his wife
and how often in the past he had been jealous of her without
any cause. Suddenly it was "don't tell." It could not be possible that he had completely forgotten her. I decided that, if he
had to hide everything about his past, perhaps it made sense
to him to conceal that he had a wife.

Now, if anyone asked, I would have to answer that
she was dead. Since I myself was listed at the institute as an
orphan, why did this disturb me so? The only answer was
that I was jealous for my mother's sake. It was not possible
for me to resign myself to the fact that another woman had
taken the place of my beloved mother, albeit not lawfully.
Thus, I said neither "yes" nor "no" to my father's request.

One day, on his day off, he invited me to go with him
to an acquaintance's home in the city. I readily agreed. We
came to a very beautiful district of Leningrad. Father knocked
on the door of an apartment, and a pleasant woman, Varvara
Nikolaevna, opened the door and invited us in.

Varvara Nikolaevna had been a widow for several
years. I understood from the conversation that her husband
had been killed in an explosion at a film factory. We were
both somewhat embarrassed. She studied me intently, and I
tried to look at her when she turned her gaze to the side.

One question intrigued me: why had my father dis-
guised the fact that this female friend was more than an acquaintance? She lived quite alone and had no children or
relatives. Evidently their loneliness united them. Yet in my
heart, insult and jealously flared violently. How could he
have done this?

Varvara Nikolaevna tried to gain my attention and
spoke especially sweetly to me. She addressed my father with
the familiar form of address, which meant they were quite
close. I became more and more depressed and silent, answering questions only when one of them addressed me directly.
Varvara understood that I did not approve of my father and
of their bond.

We parted with pleasant but superficial words. After several days Father suggested that I go with him to her place, but I refused, so he did not go either. A coldness grew between us. We didn't discuss this, but we both knew my mother was the reason for this chill.

I loved both my parents. Although I had always been close to Father, my love for Mother, a martyr and a victim of circumstance, grew from our ordeals wandering through the vast open spaces of Siberia. Suddenly, the thought of a replacement for this woman horrified me. I was ready to flare up and tell Father everything to his face, grab my decrepit suitcase, and leave. The long years of separation and the unknown restrained this impulse, but this did not mean that I resigned myself to this new situation.

I was always my father's favorite daughter, so much like him in character and appearance, but so different in views of life and circumstance. Looking back, I wonder if I was right to feel that way. How hard it is to judge others.

This was 1938. I still had one year of study left at the institute. I awaited with impatience the day when I would finish and begin to work as a teacher.

3

While still on vacation, in the early fall of 1937, I decided to visit my sister Marina. Returning from my sister's, I stopped by my brother's place.

A young teacher had arrived at the Oskaia School where my brother worked. Her name was Zoya Nikolaevna, and she charmed the entire teaching staff of the school. It was impossible to find an apartment, so my brother was letting her stay at his apartment temporarily.

My train arrived late in the evening, and I walked the kilometer to my brother's home from the station. When I entered, I noticed that someone was sleeping in my bed and that a man, covered from head to toe by a blanket, was lying near the door. Thinking he was my father, I almost threw myself on the person on the floor. I refrained, knowing that our father couldn't have come, considering all the circumstances. Boris introduced me to Zoya, and he explained that the sleeping figure on the floor was her brother Arkadii. Since there was nowhere for me to sleep, Zoya proposed I lie next to her (in my own bed).

The next morning I became acquainted with the new teacher. She had just been graduated from the geography department in the Pedagogical Institute. She was a tall, well-proportioned woman, with very beautiful facial features. Her handsome brother Arkadii was a senior lieutenant at an artillery school. Our first meeting knocked me off my feet—it was love at first sight! I studied him furtively, while he did the same to me.

We went as a group to a nearby village for apples. After lunch Arkadii and I strolled alone along the riverbank and didn't return until evening. The walk was enjoyable, and we both understood that we liked each other. Unfortunately, I had to leave and return to the institute. Arkadii implored me to stay for just one more day, but I knew I had to go.

Studies began at the institute, but a heavy weight pressed on my heart. I could not concentrate on what the professor was saying. After several days, I received a letter from Arkadii containing declarations of love. I was filled with joy. I began to receive letters from him often. He invited me to come and visit him in Smolensk. Zoya and I decided to go for several days during winter vacation.

When we arrived, Arkadii and his friend Mikhail were waiting for us at the terminal. It was wonderful seeing Arkadii again. He introduced Zoya to his friend, who was also a senior lieutenant. They had both been retained as teachers upon their graduation from school.

Upon arrival at Arkadii's apartment, we quickly changed and headed off to a cafe for a cup of tea. That evening we went to see the operetta *The Orchards Bloom*. I never thought that in Smolensk there could be such a newly built theater. I still remember words from the operetta:

> It is good, when the orchards bloom,
> It is good, when it is so sunny all around,
> It is good, when with you, my dear friend.

After the theater, we went to a restaurant in the center of the city. Most of the patrons were military officers. Arkadii asked me what I would like to drink, but as I had no experience with alcohol, he ordered Obrikotin, a liqueur, for me. My face flushed after the first sips. I became even more merry. At the end of supper Arkadii whispered to me, "Hold firmly to me when you get up, Lena."

I was offended, because I didn't feel at all intoxicated. Indeed, I had drunk only a little, but I didn't know the powerful effect of this liqueur on the legs. Again Arkadii whispered to me, "Don't let me down. Many of my friends are here."

I obeyed; when I got up, I felt the weakness in my legs. Holding onto his arm, I made it along the narrow carpet through the entire restaurant. This was my christening with alcoholic beverages.

We spent several days together. Arkadii let us have his room and spent the nights at a friend's. It was a small room, and Zoya and I slept in one bed. The kitchen was communal, and when we went out to the washstand in the morning the officers' wives looked at us suspiciously. One woman in particular, a commissar's wife, tried to start a conversation upon meeting us. Arkadii had warned us that she loved to gossip and that we were not to enter into conversation with her on any subject.

The winter vacation was too short. Zoya had to return to work, and I went back to the institute, although I really didn't want to leave.

Everything seemed very happy, as in a fairy tale. I had barely returned home when I began to receive letters. Arkadii wrote me often, called me on the telephone, and sent me flowers. I walked on air and did not feel the earth under my feet. But, as Boris had once said, "On this earth, happiness, like unhappiness, is not eternal." Everything comes to an end sometime.

In the early spring of 1939, Arkadii called and said that they would be living in military camps not far from the city of Dorogobuzh that summer. He told me, in quite an authoritative tone, to drop my studies and come to him immediately. How could I abandon that which was so important to me in life? How could I not finish my education? It was out of the question, regardless of the fact that I had fallen in love with him.

Arkadii called me again after several days, and I explained to him that his plan had to be temporarily postponed. He didn't agree with my objections and was unconvinced of my reasoning. He even threatened to come take me away, if I dared to contradict his wishes.

The conversation became very strained. Arkadii was irritated and would not listen to what I said. I could not believe that he could be so stubborn. He hung up without having said good-bye. For several days I relived this conversation and always arrived at the conclusion that my decision had been correct.

"But what if he doesn't call or write anymore?" I thought to myself.

"Well, then it means it wasn't destined," an internal voice answered.

No one would ever force me to give up my studies! After all, I had dreamed and made plans that could be realized only after graduation from the institute.

It was difficult to study and prepare for examinations in the following weeks. I wasn't able to sleep many nights and I lost weight. There was a lump in my throat, and tears welled in my eyes. I tried to control myself and told no one of my feelings. A week passed, then another, and then a month with no word from Arkadii. My heart was torn with anguish, and I even considered, briefly, abandoning everything for my beloved. "No, no! You can't be weak, you must endure even this blow," my internal voice told me.

I had to share my feelings with someone. I called my brother and asked him to come see me on Sunday. I met Boris at the terminal and burst into tears. At first he thought that I had some sort of trouble at the institute. We stopped at a cafe, and over a cup of tea I told him everything. He listened and did not take his eyes from my face.

"You, poor suffering thing! I'm very happy with your decision . . . it's logical and correct," he assured me. Boris made me promise to work seriously because it would distract me from my torment.

I looked at him as my friend and savior. Although it

was much easier to say than to do, I gradually recovered from my anguish. In the following months, I began to go out again with my girlfriends. One Sunday, Anya and I decided to wander throughout the stores and then maybe over to the cinema. The main goal of our outing was to get our pictures taken at the photo studio.

It was cloudy and drizzling a fine autumn rain. Anya and I decided to drop by the former student dining hall, not far from the institute. Lunches there were inexpensive. We stood in line to get coupons for the meal. Suddenly, almost at the cashier's window, we were surrounded by teenagers who didn't look like students. I felt a hand on my stomach, glanced down, and saw that a thief was worming his hand into an inner pocket of my overcoat. I almost shouted. The thief pulled his hand out, but three others were standing nearby, glaring at me maliciously. I knew what could happen: when the victim began to shout, the thief would use a razor to slash the face or eyes with the speed of lightning, and then disappear. I was shaking; my lips were trembling. When Anya asked what had happened, we sat at a table, and I quietly told her. The thieves still sat in the far corner of the dining hall and watched us all the time.

To distract ourselves, we began to look at our photos again, not noticing that three men had entered the dining hall. One of them immediately spotted us. We didn't even have time to put the photos back into the envelope before Evgenii, Anya's friend, came over.

"It's good you're here," Evgenii said to me. "Anton should arrive soon, and now you must meet each other."

My mood had been ruined by the thieves, so I didn't feel like staying long in the dining hall. We finished our lunches. Anya wanted very much to stay, and she tried to persuade me to wait until Anton arrived. I declined and left to prepare for lectures, but Anya stayed with Evgenii. She was crazy about him.

"Wait for some stranger?" I thought. "Why should I do that?"

Later, I found Anya brooding. "Why couldn't you have waited another ten minutes or so, Lena? Anton came, and it's a pity that you two didn't meet. I'm sure that you would like him very much."

"Why are you so sure?" I asked.

"I know your taste," she answered.

"My dear Anichka, I still haven't forgotten Arkadii."

"But he's forgotten you," she said with some irritation.

I became silent. This was throwing salt on an open wound.

That Monday after the lecture, I received a letter from Lieutenant Lomonosov. His unit was moving to a different place, and he wrote saying he would be able to come to our city to meet me. I revived a little at this welcome news. He rarely wrote, but his letters were always long and interesting. We were friendly, but he had more serious intentions. Since we could not meet often, his letters underscored his fear that he would lose me.

He did lose me later on, but not because of the rareness of our meetings. Life with a soldier would turn a woman into a roaming gypsy. This could satisfy women without a profession or education. Many military men had temporary wives in all the places where their units were transferred. On the other hand, my idea of marriage was forever, until the end of life. My brother always told me his thoughts on the matter, emphasizing that I had suffered enough and deserved a quieter harbor in life.

4

In September 1939, Soviet troops crossed the border of Poland and, under the pact with Adolph Hitler, occupied western Byelorussia and the Ukraine. That winter the war with Finland began. All male teachers, who earlier had been exempt from military service, were summoned to the military registration office and received orders to report to various military units. There were no exceptions to this decree, so Boris was taken into the army. Although he had been exempt from military service for eleven years, there was now no mercy even for him.

The authorities sent some of us last-year students to schools to replace those who were drafted. We had basically already completed all the courses and were going through student teaching. It was announced that there would be courses in the summer so that we could finish and receive our diplomas.

I received an appointment to Yazvinskaya Secondary School, approximately eighty kilometers from the city of Vitebsk. I was glad that this school was near a railroad station, since it would be possible to go to the city more often on my days off. Many of my friends were sent to out-of-the-way places, far from any means of communication, but no one could refuse an appointment.

When I arrived at the school, I immediately went to see the director, Vladimir Pavlovich Kozlov. He was an obtuse, uncultured man, with a Communist Party membership card in his pocket. His wife was the same. She was uneducated and a great gossip.

It was not pleasant to have to associate with such people. There weren't enough apartments, so I was given a small room next to the director's apartment at the school, without even a lock on the door. Another female teacher, a snoop for the director and his wife, also lived there. None of the teachers liked her, and they tried to avoid her. The remaining teachers lived in the village—some with relatives, and others in rented apartments (more accurately corners) in the huts of collective farmers. Thus began my career as a teacher.

I arrived at the school before the celebration of the October Revolution, the annual event that involved heaping praise on everything associated with the Bolsheviks' rise to power in 1917. Everyone was required to be present at the solemn ceremonies held at the school club. I sat in the first row, next to the director himself. This celebration was to be marked with a program, for which, needless to say, it was necessary to prepare oneself.

A history teacher approached the director and said, "Vladimir Pavlovich, I want to sing a song called 'The Komsomol Heart Is Broken.' "

"Absurd!" he retorted. "How can a Komsomol heart be broken? Sing something else!"

I stifled laughter, restraining myself so as not to give myself away or to show the director of the school, the defender of the Party line, how stupid I thought he was. The teacher agreed with the director's convincing arguments and began to sing another song, saving me from embarrassing giggles. In the middle of the song, he fell silent; he had forgotten the words. I couldn't suppress my laughter, although I laughed quietly to myself. The event was successful, and after everyone left, Kozlov apparently wrote a report to the higher authorities on how solemnly the day was celebrated.

The facilities of our school were in wretched condition, so a new Stalin school was built next to it.[4] I did not want to stay there but had no other place to go. Once again the situation developed in my favor.

My brother's wife was in a very difficult situation. Regardless of her cruel behavior toward me after my return from Siberia and during the times I had stayed with her, I pitied Zhenia and especially my small niece, Erochka. Since she had not worked before Boris was drafted, his mobilization left her without any means of livelihood. Without an education, it was difficult for her to find work except as a cleaning woman.

I put aside all the insults and the bitterness and began to try to get a transfer to the Oskaia School to help my brother's family financially. Teachers' salaries were meager, but it would still be better to be together and share a slice of bread than to be apart. Acquaintances with people of influence helped me to obtain a transfer to my former school as a Russian language teacher. I moved to an apartment there with my sister-in-law.

The Oskaia Secondary School was located in a beautiful place, and the school itself was very good. The director was a man of high education and culture. The contrast to my last teaching assignment was immediately evident. An amateur talent society had been organized, led by the director's wife, a sweet woman who taught zoology. I was glad to be around them and worked with great zeal. During the first quarter, the director and academic vice-president visited my classes several times. Fortunately, all went well and they praised my work.

Besides teaching language, I coached a girls' gymnastics team. The group took part in the district olympiad, won the prize, and was sent to the regional olympiad. The girls went wild with joy as they embraced and kissed me, although the real credit for the victory belonged to them. Their happy faces pleased me greatly. After the examinations, we set off for the regional olympiad, which was held in the city of Vitebsk.

A representative of the olympiad committee, who was the head of the regional Department of People's Education, met us at the terminal. He was an attractive man of about forty, very neatly dressed and pleasant. We went by tram from the terminal, and while sitting next to me he proceeded to ask me all kinds of probing questions. His interest in me was apparent. His name was Anatolii Sharralo. Although his surname was not Russian, he spoke the language beautifully. I later learned that he had been a major in the army and was forced to leave the service because of a wound.

We arrived at the dormitory. Lodgings had been specially prepared for the participants in the olympiad competitions. The beds had new snow-white sheets, blankets, and pillows. The dining hall was located in the same building. The food was excellent, by our standards. My girls were unbelievably happy. Many of them had never been in such clean conditions and had never eaten so well three times a day.

Poverty and hunger had marked my condition since our family had been exiled. The famished life as a student and even as a teacher did not cease. Because of constant shortages of food and clothing, we had only the most basic necessities. The comfortable accommodations and abundant food at the regional olympiad therefore seemed great luxuries.

The authorities even obtained uniforms for the group. This was indeed difficult since it was usually a great problem to get any clothing. The dark blue wide pants and singlets distributed to our group before the performance did not have to be returned at the end of the competition.

The girls were ecstatic. "We will never lose anywhere

as long as we have our Elena Georgievna!" my girls would say about me, their eyes shining. All of them had braided hair, with clean, tanned faces expressing goodness. I admired them, and my love and respect for them were paid in kind. They tried very hard to win one of the first places, which they did. After the regional olympiad, my group was invited to the republic olympiad in Minsk, but I could not go because of the summer courses at the institute. It was too important to me to receive a diploma.

Anatolii Sharralo, the representative of the olympiad committee who had met us at the terminal, was very nice as he tried to fulfill all our requests. The competitions ended and the participants began to leave. Anatolii and I took my girls to the terminal and put them on the train, asking the conductor to keep an eye on them. As we were returning to the city on the tram, he suggested going to the cinema that evening. I readily agreed.

That day, however, I needed to register at the institute. I met up with several of my old friends who also wanted to go to the cinema that evening. I declined and promised to go with them another time. I met Anatolii at the appointed place on the square near the watchtower, and we went to the cinema. He bought chocolate before the show. The film was interesting, and it was enjoyable to be with Anatolii.

While going out into the street after the show, I noticed several of my classmates. One of them looked intently at my companion and me and, with a smile, shook her finger at me. I did not think anything of this, simply taking this gesture as a joke. Anatolii and I walked to a restaurant and ate supper, and he accompanied me back to the Goldmans' house, where I was staying. Their daughter Roza was already married and working at the school.

The next day Anatolii invited me to go to the river for a boat ride. Since lectures at the institute had not yet started, I agreed. It was tempting to ride in a boat with such an attractive man.

Walking along the bank of the river, Anatolii took my hand and squeezed it affectionately and began to pay lavish compliments. I began to be wary. It disturbed me when he asked me why I wore a white dress. I didn't have many clothes and had worn a modest linen dress. Thinking that this was none of his business, I simply replied that in the summer people wore white clothing.

Riding in the boat on the river was great fun, and my good mood was reflected by nature. The river's banks were especially beautiful. A peculiar cautious urge echoed in my mind, however, as though something wrong would happen. We parted with a somewhat strange feeling. I did not understand why. Did I take his question as a hint, or did I intuitively sense a bad end?

The next day Anatolii sent me a huge bouquet of flowers. This was the first time in my life anyone had sent me such a beautiful bouquet. That morning, the girl who had shaken her finger at me at the cinema came up to me at the institute. She said that she knew my acquaintance Anatolii and that he was married and had a daughter. I was horrified! How dare he invite me to the cinema, take me boating, send flowers, and at the same time hide from me that he was married?

The girl who reported this unpleasant news to me was named Nina. Later she invited me to her apartment. When I arrived, I was surprised that Nina, a girl from a village, could rent a room in such a fine house. It turned out that she was Anatolii's wife's niece. That meant that Anatolii hadn't noticed her at the cinema when she had shaken her finger. Entering the house, I turned my attention to the fact that the furniture in the apartment was luxurious by our standards.

Nina met me in the corridor and took me to her room. Exactly a minute later, a young woman of about thirty came in with a curious look on her face. Extending her hand to me, she gave her name and surname: Liudmilla Sharralo. A shiver ran through my body. Although I had done her no wrong, I still blushed terribly. At this time Anatolii came out from another room, which disturbed me even more. He greeted me and, having turned to his wife, said that I was one of the participants in the olympiad competitions. I lowered my eyes, and his wife noticed my embarrassment. She invited us all to have a cup of tea and we talked about various topics. They had a daughter of about six, Verochka. Liudmilla was a member of the Communist Party and worked in a district bureau.

Liudmilla and Anatolii both behaved very calmly throughout the conversation. I was the only one apparently feeling any embarrassment in this situation. I later learned that Liudmilla had lovers and was unfaithful to her husband at every opportunity. Nina was not particularly disturbed that Anatolii met with different women. Although from the beginning I had been quite indifferent to Anatolii, his attention to my girls and me had impressed me. I nevertheless decided that their lifestyle was their business and that I would not allow myself to become enmeshed in such a situation.

Although I felt as if life had failed me, I endured this breakup, too. The memory of each broken romance did not disappear entirely. I went proudly forward, anyway, in search of my dream. These experiences only underlined once again that life itself is like the ocean waves, which lash and try to swallow you with their strength and carry you away into the depths. If a person's strength of will is weak, then it goes without saying that she will disappear into the waves.

CHAPTER THREE

SHORTLIVED JOY

1

It was already 1940, after the division of Poland and during the war with Finland. The smell of war was in the air, in spite of the treaty with Germany. The cities were full of soldiers, and, although no one dared voice feelings aloud, the general population was anxious about the approaching catastrophe. The notion of war terrified everyone, especially mothers.

The stores were empty, as usual. Only in a good restaurant was it possible to enjoy adequate food. These restaurants were occupied by those who could afford such luxuries. I had already worked for a year and had received money in advance for the summer months, so I was feeling rich and decided to go out to eat. Since Anya had gone home to the country after the lectures on Friday, I stopped by our favorite restaurant alone.

There wasn't a single available space when I entered. Looking around the restaurant, I saw my former professor of Byelorussian literature, who loved to chase after his female students. He was always neatly and elegantly dressed, but his face was very ugly and we called him "frog face." Several times he had invited me to go with him to the cinema or the theater, but I had always managed to find a reason to decline. This meeting was unexpected, and when he asked if I would join his group of about six I had no choice but to accept. The professor sat to my right. On my left was a man I had never met. The professor introduced me to his friends, but, to my embarrassment, I didn't remember any of their names.

I chidingly asked them why their wives hadn't prepared lunch for them, and they responded by asking me why I hadn't done the same for my husband. Our marital status thus disclosed, we went on to other subjects. My former professor began to talk about my scholastic abilities, and I blushed with modesty. The conversation continued about me, where I worked, and what subjects I taught. Then the man on my left asked if I knew Anya.

"She's my best friend," I answered.

"And I'm a good friend of her friend Evgenii," he mentioned. I pricked up my ears.

"You are Anton?" I asked him, not without curiosity.

"Yes, and you are Lena? I've tried to meet you several times, but unsuccessfully. It seems I've known you for a whole year. It's like being acquainted without seeing you."

Turning more to his side, I looked him over stealthily: gray, expressive eyes in a handsome face framed with dark, smoothly combed hair. He was tall, broad-shouldered, and dressed tastefully in a dark gray suit.

We became increasingly absorbed in our own conversation and, to some degree, ignored the others who were sitting at the table. We talked about many things, such as music and the latest records by Kozlovskii and Lemeshev. When we had finished eating, Anton asked me where I had my apartment. It was not far from his school. Saying good-bye to our companions, we left the restaurant. It was somewhat hot, but we decided to go on foot.

Sometimes when a woman and a man meet and start to talk, they have so little in common that confusion and silence punctuate the conversation, but this was not the case with Anton and me. We reached my apartment hardly without noticing. We finally stopped but continued to talk. Neither he nor I wanted to break the pleasant moment and say good-bye. Anton asked if I would go to the cinema with him that evening, and I, of course, agreed without hesitation. My face could not hide my pleasure. We parted.

When I entered the apartment, my landlady said to me in a whisper that Lieutenant Lomonosov was waiting for me, even though his regiment was some distance from my place. He had come from the terminal a while before and had fallen asleep on the couch.

"What shall I do now?" I frantically asked myself. "I've got a date with Anton, and I don't want to offend him." There were no private telephones, so I couldn't call and postpone. He wouldn't receive a note in time. Besides, I didn't know his home address. I approached Alexander on tiptoe and was going to touch his shoulder when he opened his eyes.

"Oh! I must have dozed off," he said. "Pardon me, Lenochka! I didn't sleep all night. It was noisy in the train car. A large group of soldiers rode with me, and I have to report at the regiment today. Let me wash and then we will go someplace."

The landlady brought a towel from her room. The washstand hung on the wall behind a partition in a corner of the kitchen. Alexander came from behind the partition with a fresher face and smoothly brushed hair.

"What a pleasant and restrained man he is," I thought to myself. "How well the military uniform suits him!"

He interrupted my thoughts: "What plans do you have for tomorrow, Lena? I must report my arrival to the regiment today, but I think I will be free tomorrow, and we can spend time together."

I was relieved. There was no need to worry about my meeting with Anton that evening. Alexander and I spent the afternoon together in a nearby park. When it came time for him to leave so he could be at the military base before nightfall, we agreed to meet as soon as he was given the opportunity.

That evening Anton and I went to the cinema. I was unusually silent and gave brief answers to Anton's questions. After the film we went on foot toward my apartment. He pressed my hand firmly and tried to look me in the face. Noticing my distraction, he asked, "Is something bothering you? Did I say something wrong?"

"Oh, no," I replied. "I'm just a little tired and am thinking about my courses."

"When can I see you again?" Anton asked, troubled.

"I can't tomorrow, I'm busy. Maybe the day after to-morrow," I answered.

Alexander was not given leave from his regiment for an entire week. He sent me a short letter in which he apologized and wrote that he would very much like to see me more often. But business before pleasure, he concluded.

During this time, my sister Marina was vacationing with her children in the country at the home of her in-laws, while her husband Peter was in Leningrad on temporary duty. Marina decided to surprise me and came to visit. I was very glad to see her. While we were visiting in my room, Anton came by and knocked on my window, which faced the street. I raised the curtain a bit and opened the window. His arrival surprised me. After all, we had agreed to meet at seven o'clock that evening.

He hastened to explain that there was a good play at the theater and that if I wanted to go he would get tickets. I invited him to come into the apartment and introduced him to my sister and the landlady. A samovar was hissing on the table, and we invited him to have a cup of tea with us. He declined graciously. Turning to Marina he asked, "Can I invite you to join Lena and me to go to the theater?"

"With great pleasure!" she responded enthusiastically. "I am tired of sitting in the country feeding the mosquitoes. I'm drawn to the city, so I came to visit Lena without telling her," she added.

"Excellent! I'll go get the tickets right now," Anton replied. "I'm very glad to have met you, and I'll see you both this evening."

Marina immediately turned to me with approval and expressed her opinion of him: "He is a very courteous and pleasant man. See for yourself, but in my opinion he suits you very well. He is handsome and evidently very kind and attentive." "Don't pursue officers," she added.

I only smiled in reply. I knew that by "officers" she meant Alexander Lomonosov. The majority of young girls pursued pilots and lieutenants and clung to them closely. Officers were more materially secure than civilians. They received apartments without any problems and could buy food at reduced prices in restricted stores. A teacher, on the other hand, could only get books, notebooks, a meager salary, and an overload of work.

In those hard times, one had to stand in long lines for kerosene or any kind of food, be it bread, margarine, flour, or cornmeal. Hectic work schedules prevented waiting in line many times. We also went to the flea market, where it was sometimes possible to buy vegetables, chicken, or a piece of salt pork. No one dared complain of the hardship. It was necessary to express delight at all times and thank the Communist Party for a fortunate and joyful life.

While we were getting ready for the theater, I saw that Marina wanted me to look especially good.

"Why have you grown taller than I, Lenok? You could have worn my chiffon dress, but it's too short for you. I want to see you well-dressed and stylish." My sister was prettier than I but quite a bit shorter. She often would say to me, "If I had my face, but your height . . ."

When we were both dressed, we set off for the theater. My landlady made the sign of the cross over us both with a motion of her hand and quietly whispered something.

I, too, addressed myself to God secretly. I had prayed since earliest childhood, influenced by my grandmother and mother. I had composed my own tearful prayers in Siberia and during the escape. I had prayed over my dying mother and in my prayers remembered my father daily. I prayed and asked the Lord to turn our enemies away from us, our persecutors who haunted us at every step and from whom we couldn't hide. So why did it surprise me that the landlady made the sign of the cross over us, I asked myself mentally.

When we got off the tram at the square near the theater, Anton was already waiting for us with a delighted smile. We all entered the foyer together. Anton asked us if we wouldn't like to drink something or to eat a pastry. We declined. After the first bell we went into the theater and took our seats. Anton sat between my sister and me. On my side, along the aisle, was an empty seat. After the third bell, just before the beginning of the performance, a man hurriedly sat down. At first I paid no attention, but then I inadvertently turned in his direction and to my horror saw it was Anatolii Sharralo, without his wife.

"Good evening, Lena!" said Anatolii.

"Good evening, Anatolli," I answered quietly, my face blushing unbelievably. Turning to Anton's side, I was going to introduce them to each other, but it turned out that they already knew each other officially through their jobs. I introduced Marina, who already knew all about Anatolii. My mood was spoiled by this unexpected meeting. Anton noticed my embarrassment and asked me where I had met Sharralo. I told him the circumstances of our acquaintance and changed the subject.

The actors' performances were excellent, although Soviet propaganda had been deeply injected into the work, as prescribed by law. The theater, the cinema, and all aspects of artistic expression had to meet the demands of socialist realism. This resulted in portrayals of devoted Party members and happy, productive workers, discussing the merits of socialism over capitalism. This play was about how spies and traitors were everywhere, and how the arm of the law skillfully repressed them. During the performance, I involuntarily recalled the authorities' accusations against my father and thousands like him. I felt an incredible weight on my heart and became preoccupied and unhappy. How I would have liked to forget the past, never to remember all the suffering.

After the performance we decided to walk home. I became even more quiet along the way. Marina carried on all of the conversation with Anton, who kept looking at me. He accompanied us to my apartment and left. I don't know if it was the meeting with Anatolii or the spurious theme of the play that spoiled my mood more.

Hearing obvious lies such as those in the play made me reflect on the past and ask myself the same questions: Who needs these guiltless victims? Who gave those in power, elected by no one, the right to command the fates of millions? Who are these people? Do they have any feeling of compassion and respect for others? Why is there such cruelty and tyranny? Hundreds of similar questions crowded my head. Even thinking them was dangerous, and it was strictly forbidden to ask them aloud. Besides that, who could you ask? The nation was reduced to sufferers and the silent.

I will never forget one time when they reported over the loudspeaker a new decree of the Party and government: the introduction of strict discipline in all branches of socialist construction, which mainly meant that one would be punished for being more than ten minutes late. Hearing this decree, I thought to myself with bitter irony: "It has become better and more wonderful to live, comrades." This frightened me, and I immediately tried to distract myself.

The day after Anton took us to the theater, my sister and I went to the big department store GUM. As always, the high prices of all the goods were startling. I very much liked the crêpe-de-chine fabric, which cost 105 rubles a meter, but I would have to pay from 80 to 100 rubles for the labor to have a dress sewn, making the total cost more than 400 rubles. This was a teacher's monthly pay. Women's shoes in GUM were 450 rubles. Who could buy such things? At special distributors for the Soviet elite, such shoes cost 100 rubles. At least it was nice to look at some lovely things since, except for GUM, the other stores were completely empty. After we strolled along the streets for some time, Marina and I became quite hungry. We entered a cafe, had some tea with pastries, and returned home.

That evening Marina had to return to the country. She already missed her children. It was very enjoyable to have spent this short time with her. Although we were different in nature, I valued her sharp mind. She treated me tenderly and strove to help me as much as she was able. Leaving for the country, she made me promise that I would visit her, and I agreed gladly.

When I came home from work at the institute one day some months later, I found a letter from my brother. He scolded me for never writing to him of his wife's behavior. One of our teachers apparently had reported to him all about her escapades and her meetings with various lovers. Yes, I had known of all this, but I had no desire to cause my own brother grief. We all knew that he had never loved her and that the only thing that bound him to her was their daughter Erochka.

After Boris had been drafted into the army and I moved in with his wife and daughter, I witnessed more of her behavior. During one fling, she consorted with a peat factory technician who had a wife and six children. People verified what I saw, but what could I do?

On one of her periodic trips to the bazaar in the nearest city to buy groceries, she met a Red Army soldier on the train. I would never have learned of this meeting, if not for her carelessness: she wore my jacket when she went to the post office and put the receipt for a registered letter she had sent in the pocket.

The answer to this letter came a few days later. When the postman gave me the mail, there were letters from my brother to her and to me. There was also a third letter, which provoked my curiosity. The address was written in poor handwriting, and a military postmark was on the envelope. I gave her both letters.

While opening it, she unwittingly let a small photo of a man fall under the table. Reading hurriedly, she didn't notice that he had mentioned the photo in the letter. Later, while sweeping the floor after lunch, I retrieved the photo from under the table. I was outraged when I looked at it. I gave it to her, not without sarcasm. She burst out with verbal abuse, accusing me of having opened her letter.

"That's absurd!" I said. "I wasn't raised to open other people's letters."

Putting my jacket on, I went for water from the well. I automatically put my hand into the pocket and discovered a paper, which was the receipt. Entering the apartment, trying to be as calm as I could, I held the receipt out to her, recommending that she not lose such things. Even though I caught her red-handed, I dared not tell my brother of this. What would be gained? Life was difficult enough for him.

Once, in a conversation with Mother, Boris hinted that he wanted to divorce Zhenia. Mother was appalled and told him authoritatively: "There have been no divorces in our family . . . you didn't ask us when you married her, and now, my dear son, don't ask for my blessing to a divorce." Boris became silent and never again spoke with anyone on this subject.

In spite of his unhappy marriage, Boris was attentive to the needs of his family and was never unfaithful to his wife. It hurt me to see how she repaid his devotion. The state gave a small pittance to those they had called up but gave no help at all to their families, since the duty of every citizen was to serve the Party, the government, and the Motherland. I gave all the money I could to my sister-in-law. Marina also helped her. Zhenia still could not make ends meet.

Having learned all about her adventures, Boris asked his superiors for two weeks' leave. He arrived home for his surprise visit one Saturday. Alexander had come to see me, and we were standing on the street near my apartment deciding how to spend the day. Masses of people were on the streets. Because you could always see soldiers in the crowds, I paid no attention to the man in military uniform who was approaching us. As he came closer, I recognized my brother, whom I had never before seen in uniform. Saluting Alexander, Boris introduced himself.

Boris was sad. He had only a short time to be home, but first he wanted to speak with me. I excused myself to Alexander and promised to meet him the next day. At this point, I could not avoid telling my brother everything that I knew about his wife. He knew even more than I did since someone else already had informed him in letters.

"Boris," I said, "you have always told me to be logical, not to act impulsively, and not to be guided by my heart but to think with my head." I looked him directly in the eye and told him to weigh all the circumstances. Yet I still wanted to lessen his pain. We headed for the terminal so that Boris could return home quickly, see Erochka, and find a solution to this complicated situation as soon as possible. On the way home from the terminal, I prayed in my soul, asking for help in this unpleasant situation.

Boris nevertheless was thinking about me and asked about Alexander Lomonosov.

"How serious are your intentions?" he asked, not looking at me.

"It can't be at all serious. He is very kind and dear, but I'm not thinking of a serious decision at this time," I responded. In other words, I liked him but was not in love. In fact, after his last visit, I never saw Alexander again. He stopped by one last time but I was not home. I think my landlady must have said something to him. Even if he had been transferred unexpectedly to another city, he would have let me know. Thus the end of my relationship with him came about with no particular hard feelings.

"What happened to Arkadii?" Boris continued.

"Oh! He married and has already managed to get divorced." His marriage was only a response to my refusal to leave the institute and go to him on his orders. "You know about this, Boris . . . I told you all about it when you came to see me. Now I'm interested in Anton, a mathematics teacher and the academic vice-president at the secondary school." Besides filling long hours with his duties as a teacher and academic vice-president, Anton was also the inspector of the Pervomaiskii school district.

"I like him, and Marina approves of my choice," I added.

Seeing firsthand the families of military men, Boris seriously advised me to stay as far away from them as possible. Because Anton was following an academic instead of a military path, Boris was on his side without having met him. The counsel of Boris and Marina, and especially my feelings toward Anton, influenced me.

Boris was recalled to his regiment on the second day of his leave. His assistant had muddled something, so they sent him a telegram that simply ordered his return. Boris was not able to resolve his family problems. He later wrote me that when he arrived, he embraced Erochka, but didn't even greet his wife.

Zhenia begged his forgiveness, but regardless of his usual kindheartedness he could not. She then invented accusations about me, to which he sharply replied, "You aren't worthy of being the sole of my sister's shoe! She helps you and gives up her last kopeks for you. But even knowing all the dirt about you, she still defends you and asks me to be lenient! You are a fallen woman," he added coldly. "Find yourself a job and do what you want! Lena will only help you because of Erochka."

With that, Boris returned to his military duty.

2

Anton and I began to meet more frequently, which made me very happy. Often, sitting in an auditorium listening to a lecture, I would think of him and want to see him as soon as possible.

"What is this? Can I really be in love?" I asked myself.

"Yes, oh yes," was the answer.

One evening we were supposed to go to the amphitheater for an operetta, but a heavy rain began, and we had to change our plans. Knowing that proper girls didn't go to bachelors' apartments, Anton took a chance anyway and shyly asked me if I wanted to listen to his records or hear him play the guitar. He had more than two hundred records of the newest and best music. He also played the guitar and sang well. He and I had already been dancing several times. He danced excellently and tried to teach me, even though I was a poor dancer.

Blushing brightly, I answered affirmatively. Anton was always proper and never said or did anything to offend or alarm me. Even now, when we were alone, his conduct was exceedingly correct.

His apartment was on the third floor at the secondary school and consisted of one small room and a kitchen that he never used. The school watchman had built his own workshop in this kitchen. When I entered, the cleanliness and order struck me. I immediately suspected that he was probably married, since I assumed a man could not be so neat. The music and a small glass of brandy cheered me again.

"What are your plans for the future?" he asked suddenly.

"What do you have in mind?" I replied. "I want to work and to travel about Russia, to see new places and to learn more of the Motherland."

"Don't you have dreams of building your life, of getting married?"

"Oh, yes; those dreams live in every woman's thoughts," I answered without any hesitation.

"No doubt you have many admirers, and it's hard for you to make a choice," he said, not looking at me.

I hesitated a little, as if searching for an answer. "There have been and there are now, but I'm not in a hurry. I want to find a man who will be close to me, with whom I can spend my life to the end. I don't recognize divorces. In my opinion that is too heavy a blow in life, and I've already endured enough blows. I want peace, love, and respect."

Anton was silent. I also became silent and turned my gaze to the side. I noticed a photograph of a very beautiful blonde on the upper shelf of the bookcase, but out of politeness I didn't ask who she was. Our conversation changed course.

The hours flew quickly. The rain stopped, and it was time for me to return home. We went out to the street, which was fresh and pleasant after the rain. A few clouds sailed high in the sky, like orphans left behind from a large parent cloud. "Lord! What a wonderful world!" I exclaimed to myself. "What beauty! Why don't I have wings to rise up and fly through the orphan-clouds?" After all, I was also in a way an orphan.

Such feelings usually saddened me, but, walking next to Anton, I wanted to embrace the whole world. Anton held my hand firmly as I alternated between sad and happy emotions. I wanted so much to hug him and let him know how wonderful he was and how happy I was to know him. Excessive modesty and fear restrained this impulse, for I didn't know what he would think if I expressed my feelings too quickly.

He must have read my mind, for he turned, embraced me, and for the first time in all these weeks kissed me. We didn't want to part, but we had to. Saying good night, Anton didn't even ask me if he could see me the next day. He simply said, "Tomorrow at seven in the evening on the square, near the window where they put up the papers under glass every day for the public."

I couldn't say either yes or no. Needless to say, my answer could not have been negative. I did not sleep at all that night. Anton's dear face was before my eyes all the time and thoughts of him churned in my head. How could I have been carried away by him so quickly? After all, I knew nothing about him, and he knew nothing about me. This was going on the third week of our joyful daily meetings. I no longer experienced feelings of awkwardness and fear, and more often after supper or the cinema we listened together to his music and danced.

One evening after a film we dropped by his apartment for a short while. When I was leaving, he put on a record. I don't remember who performed the song, but its words are engraved in my memory:

> Our little corner is never crowded for us;
> When you are in it, spring blossoms there.
> Don't leave, so many songs are still unsung,
> Each string of the guitar still rings.

How timely these words were. For me spring had actually come! I didn't really feel like leaving.

"Lenochka, I want to call you *ty* now. Enough of *vy*.[1] I love you, my dear! I want to share every minute with you! Every hour! All my life! I never thought that I could come to love someone so quickly! Be mine forever! Give me only one word, that you agree to marry me." He hugged me so tightly that it was difficult for me even to breathe.

"My dear Antok! Do you know who you want for a wife? You don't know my past, and you don't in fact know anything about me." These words alarmed him a little, but I tried to allay his fears.

"This does not concern my morals," I reassured him, "for I have never been intimate with a man. I need you to tell me you won't reject me if I reveal my secret to you."

"Never! Never!" Anton exclaimed. "I've told you that I can't live without you and that you are always in my thoughts. It's hard for me to concentrate on my work."

I took a breath and told him the whole truth about myself. He listened carefully to my story. I hid nothing of my life from him, starting with childhood and ending with Siberia.

"Thank you for your honesty and trust in me. I will love and respect you even more. You are a martyr and victim," he said, with a serious face.

I later learned of his family and that he was also concealing his past. His father had been a cattle breeder at a large collective farm. The livestock were in terrible shape, because there wasn't sufficient winter feed or any bedding. As a result, many cows died. The authorities arrested Anton's father and demanded a confession at the interrogation that he was a spy working for some capitalist country. When he was ordered to sign such a confession, he categorically refused. The NKVD investigator beat him to death with the butt of his pistol.

Following his father's murder, Anton had to make choices. If he admitted that his father had been persecuted, the doors of an education would be closed to him. He decided to leave his family, go to the Ukraine, and get a job in a coal mine. Since the authorities held this category of workers in esteem, Anton was able to attend a workers' school in the evenings. Directing all his energies to entering the university, he eventually succeeded and enrolled in the department of physics and mathematics, without any hindrances or certification of his social origin. Work as a coal miner obliterated one's past.

Despite the many good and great people in our country, there were so many monsters and beasts, to whom it gave pleasure to destroy guiltless human beings! This reality bothered Anton as much as it did me.

Having told each other all about ourselves, we hugged and vowed to love one another and to be inseparable forever.

"Won't you stay with me?" asked Anton.

"No, I'll stay with you when we lawfully formalize our marriage," was my answer.

"Then when will we be able to go to the ZAGS?"[2] he asked. We agreed to be married on the twenty-fifth of July.

I told my landlady of my decision. This poor woman, a widow for many years, rented me a room while she slept in a tiny corner. She survived by standing in long lines, buying a few things, and reselling them at the flea market. Many ended up in prison for speculation, but she was lucky. A devout woman, she loved me as her own daughter. She was very pleased when I told her that I was to marry Anton and confessed that she had told Alexander not to waste his time with me since I was obviously becoming serious with Anton.

How I wished that my relatives could be present at this celebration, but this was impossible. When Anton and I were ready to go, my landlady made the sign of the cross over both of us and kissed us. "Let this be a substitute for a family blessing," she said tearfully.

The registration of the marriage was the simplest of ceremonies. A very fat middle-aged woman sat at a wooden table. She asked for first name, patronymic, and surname; the year and place of birth; and nationality. Finally, she asked whether I wanted to keep my maiden name or to change to my husband's surname. I preferred to change my surname. We both signed the completed form. Anton paid the three rubles, and the whole ceremony was concluded.

We went out to the street, and I burst into a torrent of tears.

"You haven't changed your mind, Lenochka?" asked Anton worriedly.

"Oh, no, no!" I assured him. A wave of nostalgia overcame me with memories of all my parents' plans for their daughters. Now there were neither parents nor relatives, and I became melancholy. Anton tried to change my mood by talking of his upcoming leave and of the trip we planned to his mother's.

Anton had six older sisters. He was the youngest in the family. One of his sisters lived in Minsk with her own family. When he informed her and his mother of our arrival, he also told them he was coming not alone, but with his wife. He hadn't written anything about me to them. They didn't know where I was from or what my occupation was.

I also had to ask permission at work for a transfer. Even though marriage was a valid reason, there were great difficulties in receiving permission for a relocation from one place to another. Before our departure, I went to present my application. Entering the office, I told the secretary that I wished to see Anatolii Sharralo. At first she asked me why I wished to speak with him, but when I answered that it was a personal matter, she opened the door to his office to ask if he could receive me. He rose from his desk and came out to the office.

"Lena! What are you doing here?"

"I've come on business, on very important business," was my reply. A smile flitted across his face. He apparently thought that this was only a pretext on my part and that I had come simply to see him.

Anatolii invited me to go with him to the workers' dining hall to have lunch together. I thanked him but declined.

"I haven't time. My husband is waiting for me; we intend to take a trip."

"A husband! How dare you get married without my permission?" he asked with a smile.

"As you see, I dared!"

"Who is your husband?"

"You are acquainted with him; you saw him at the theater."

"You married the teacher? I never thought that you would take such a stupid step."

"Why is it stupid? Be so kind as to write out the order for my transfer," I said evenly.

"Not a chance!" he snorted.

"Are you joking?" I asked indignantly.

He didn't answer. I handed him my application, which he then and there approved and gave it to the typist.

"At which secondary school do you intend to work?"

"I still don't know."

He took a folder from the desk and leafed through the pages for a long time, then said that several schools were in need of teachers with my specialty, including the school where my husband was working.

I thought that was strange and wondered why Anton hadn't mentioned this. Sharralo recommended to me a school in a very beautiful district of the city, not far from a park, to which a tram line ran. He even wrote a short note, placed it in an envelope, and sealed it. This note was addressed to the director of the school. Since the director and academic vice-president for my new school could not be found during the summer vacation, I had to postpone seeing them until after my trip to visit Anton's family.

On the way home I was still troubled that Anton hadn't told me of the opening at his school. I hid my displeasure and decided not to raise the question with him.

I wanted to go to see my sister Marina in the country before we left. Neither she nor anyone else in my family knew about my marriage. I could only stay for the day, so I decided to take the earliest morning train. Anton dropped me off at the terminal at five o'clock in the morning and promised to meet me at eleven o'clock that evening.

Because Marina didn't know I was coming, I asked an employee at the station for directions to the village and slowly walked the four kilometers, deep in thought. With each step I recalled different events of my life, the good times and the hardships. I reflected on various people I had met and the memories they kindled. I particularly thought about a young man whom I knew while still in secondary school. His name was Efim Klesov. He was an intelligent young man, and all his grades were excellent in every subject. He was accepted by the Leningrad Air Force Academy upon completion of secondary school. We exchanged letters all the time.

My last meeting with Efim took place when I visited my father in Leningrad in 1938. It was not a joyful reunion. When he was a cadet at the academy, a terrible incident occurred that scarred him for life. While he stood guard during the celebration of the anniversary of the October Revolution, his commander, who was drunk, decided to check on how the sentry was fulfilling his duties. He knocked out a window and was going to crawl through it to someplace outside where no one, except for the top commanders and guards, was allowed to go. When Efim shouted, "Halt! Who goes there?" no answer followed. "Halt! I'll shoot!" Efim warned, only to be met with silence. A shot rang out, and the drunken commander was killed on the spot.

No punishment at all was given to Efim, but the feeling that he had killed a man gave him no peace by day or by night. Efim couldn't cope with his courses and saw no alternative but to leave the academy.

When I went to Leningrad to see my father, I called

the academy and asked the duty officer to tell Efim that I wanted to see him. Several days later he came to where my father worked and found me in the dormitory. I could not believe that this was the same Efim. He was thin, ill, and filled with grief. He wore a military uniform, which can often transform a man, but it didn't flatter him. He told me what had happened, and I gradually began to calm him and persuade him that his self-loathing was not justified.

"But I killed a man!" he kept saying.

"Yes, but you didn't want to kill him; you felt no malice, but only fulfilled your duty. What would have happened if you had not reacted to his idea to test you? He had no right to be drunk and to pull such a stunt."

Our conversation lasted for a long time. My father came to the dormitory, and I introduced them. They each drank a small glass of vodka and had a bite to eat. My father was a great joker and made Efim laugh with his anecdotes. Evening approached, and Efim had to return to the academy. I accompanied him to the tram. The correspondence between us continued after I returned to the institute.

Later, when the war began, Efim's airplane was shot down over Finland. While trying to parachute down, he was struck and killed by machine gun fire while still in the air. I learned of this from his close friend, who was in that same raid. Thus Efim, an honest, kind, people-loving man, perished.

I also thought of Arkadii and wondered where he was now, how he lived, and whether he liked his career. I knew that he had been married, if only for three weeks.

Enveloped by such recollections, as if bidding farewell to my past while entering a new life, I reached the village where Marina was spending the summer with her in-laws. A pitiable woman of medium height, with white flashes of skin among the creases of her deeply tanned, wrinkled face, wandered near a ramshackle hut. She was barefoot, her feet scratched, and her heels deeply cracked. Her clothing was old, rumpled, and dirty. Her eyes reflected sadness and fatigue.

I hurried toward her to ask where the Zanegins lived. She pointed to another hut at the far end of the village. Mud and cow and horse dung were everywhere. The collective farmers' dwellings were in poor condition. The fences were broken. This was the result of the Soviet government's decree that peasants were to be forced off their own lands onto collective farms.

Approaching the place where my sister lived, I saw my nephew and niece on the grass in the garden and ran to them. Marina came out of the house and ran over to me. The children were wary since they seldom saw me and knew little of me.

"Here's a pleasant surprise!" said Marina.

"I'm so glad to see you and the children," I answered.

"For how many days have you come?"

"For only one day. I'm leaving at ten o'clock this evening."

"Why so quickly?"

"Oh, Marina, I have some news to tell you!"

"What?"

"Guess!"

"Don't torture me! Tell!" my sister implored me.

"I've gotten married," I said in a quiet voice.

"To whom?" she said in a trembling voice.

"To Anton. We were with him at the theater. Do you remember?"

"Thank God! I like him very much." Having said this, she turned her face from me, and just then I noticed how she had grown quiet and wiped away tears.

"Why are you crying?" I asked.

"I'm crying because you have suffered so much in life, and we all wanted you to be happy." Marina then asked whether I had written to Mother (who was at this time living with her daughter-in-law) and whether Boris knew.

"No, no one knows; you are the first one I've told this news."

The day passed very quickly. We talked nonstop. No one bothered us. My sister's mother-in-law was already an elderly, sick woman, and her father-in-law worked on the collective farm as an accountant. He was away from home entire days. My sister's children slept after dinner. The day came to an end too quickly, and Marina accompanied me to the station to catch the evening train.

In the train car I thought the whole time of my sister and her lovely children, not at all noticing that the train was approaching the city where my husband was waiting for me. He met me at the terminal, and we went home slowly on foot along Vokzal'naia Street. I was pensive and sad, but Anton didn't ask me why and only glanced at me questioningly.

I did not know whether my melancholy was caused by a premonition of something bad or by reliving memories of the past. Although I did not know it at the time, this was to be my last reunion with my sister. None of us thought then that such events would unfold that we would not be able to see one another or know of each other's fates. This last meeting was joyful and brought us still closer, as if we had a presentiment of the separation forever.

3

We awoke about eight the morning after my visit with Marina and began to discuss our trip to visit Anton's mother. As he had already bought the train tickets, we only needed to put our things into a suitcase.

"And when will you bring over your things from your former apartment?" my husband asked me.

"What things?" I had already brought them over. I owned very little, but he didn't realize how little I had. Anton burst into laughter when I showed him my possessions.

The next day we were on the road to Anton's relatives. He was attentive and tender toward me. I hoped to myself that he would always be so affectionate.

The train arrived at Minsk early in the morning, and his sister Viktoriia met us at the terminal. She threw herself at her brother in an embrace and then turned toward me, inspecting me from head to toe. I could tell she approved of her brother's choice, since she was very nice to me. We rode the tram from the terminal to her place. I liked this city. The center was clean with much greenery and many flowers. Entering the apartment, we noticed that the table was already set for breakfast.

To Anton's six sisters, there was no girl who would have been good enough to marry their brother. While at the university, Anton had had a girlfriend named Yadviga who was descended from a family formerly of the Polish gentry. Everyone in his family knew her and was favorably inclined to her, mainly because she was Catholic. It was her photograph I saw when I visited Anton's apartment for the first time. That photograph disappeared, and I quickly forgot about it. Yadviga loved Anton, and they had agreed to marry as soon as they had saved some money. Like Anton, Yadviga was a mathematics teacher; after they graduated from the university, they were sent to different places to work. There was frequent correspondence between them. Suddenly Anton married another, a completely unknown girl!

Viktoriia and all the rest of the sisters loved their brother, the youngest in the family, very much. Viktoriia was particularly kind to me. Her husband was already at his work as a bookkeeper in a factory when we arrived, but her two daughters seemed very sweet and immediately began to call me Aunt Lena, which touched me very much.

After breakfast, Victoriia took us around and showed us the city. Anton already knew the city well because he had studied at the university. I was very interested, since it was my first time there.

That evening we were to leave for Anton's mother's home in a small town forty kilometers from the center of Minsk. A younger daughter and her family lived with Anton's mother. The young woman's husband managed a restaurant, and they lived well. They also had two children, a son and a daughter, who were well brought up.

Anton and I arrived at about midnight, exhausted after the two-day trip. Although my health was almost restored, I still became tired quickly. Now only red spots—traces of frostbite suffered in Siberia—appeared on my face in heat and cold. My hands and feet periodically swelled up, especially from fatigue.

Anton's mother, an old woman, had not gone to bed. Peering through the darkness and at last seeing us arrive, she rushed to her son. Crying silently, she was unable to release him from her embrace for a long time.

"Mama," Anton finally said, "this is my wife Elena. I hope that you will love her when you have gotten to know her."

I went to her and kissed her. "I'm glad to see you, Mama. Your son is dear to me; thank you for him!" My voice trembled, and I could find no more words to win her over to me.

"If you love one another, I will love you both. May God bless you for long years of life together." She took a small crucifix from her neck and brought it to Anton's lips. He crossed himself in the Catholic fashion. She then turned toward me. Crossing myself, I kissed the small crucifix.

"Are you Orthodox?"

"Yes, and I believe in God," I answered quietly.

I could tell that in her heart she would have wanted her daughter-in-law to be of their faith. Pensiveness crossed her face, and she said quickly, "The first thing that I would like is for you to go to the cemetery and kneel at your father's grave and ask for his blessing. Your father dreamed of the wedding of his son, whom he adored, but his life was taken away wrongfully. Thank God only for the fact that his body was given to us, and we were able to bury him in a cemetery, that he was not thrown somewhere in a mass grave, like thousands of other victims." She began to sob loudly.

"Forgive me, children! I am glad to see my son and take you, Elena, as my daughter. Take care of my son; he is kind, he has never harmed anyone, and I am sure that he will never harm you. I hope that you, too, will never leave him." Turning to Anton, she asked, "Why did you marry such a young and beautiful girl?"

Anton began to laugh and answered jokingly, "And why not? I am beautiful too."

"You know how family life is now," she continued. "People change husbands, they change wives all the time."

Anton's mother had borne six daughters, and Anton had been the last joyful event in her life. She doted upon him. Joy lit her face when she saw our life together, full of love and respect for one another. She had suffered greatly when Anton was forced to leave his family home to go into the unknown after his father's tragic death.

Anton felt deep regret but said nothing aloud when he learned of his sisters' misfortunes, which had befallen one after another. His eldest sister's husband, an engineer, had been shot and killed on his own doorstep in front of his wife and children. The only charge against this guiltless man was that he had an "intelligent mug." The husbands of two other sisters had been arrested, and their fates were still unknown. The wives' efforts to find their husbands were met with rudeness and threats. "We have no such person here—go to a higher office," they were told.

Having finished asking about our lives, Anton's mother invited us to eat. We declined, since I could hardly stay on my feet or even hold my eyes open.

It was very stuffy in the house, but we could not open a window, because thousands of mosquitoes would fill the house. The house consisted of two buildings, joined by a large hallway. The mother lived in one part, Anton's sister in the other. The windows of one building looked out onto the fruit garden. In the yard was a large barn, also consisting of two sections. The domestic livestock were located in one section, and in the other section were the hay, straw, and implements. Everything was in good order. We decided to go sleep in the barn, where it was cool and scented by fragrant hay. I fell asleep almost before my head touched the pillow.

When I awoke late in the morning, Anton was already out of bed. I entered the house to find the whole family assembled: his sister, her husband, their children.

"It seems I've slept too long! Why didn't you wake me, Anton?"

"Why?" he answered and, turning to his sister and her husband, he introduced me. I kissed both of them and their children.

We sat down to breakfast. At first an awkward silence reigned at the table.

"Mama, Lena has also traveled a difficult path," Anton said. "She was banished with her parents to Siberia."

He told of my ordeal without unnecessary details. Hearing of my past, the whole family was won over to me.

We then talked of how to gather all the relatives for a wedding for us. We decided to write invitations to everyone immediately.

The family doubted that the eldest sister, Mariia, would be able to come, because she lived far away. She had four children. Like Anton, they had left their family home and scattered to cover the traces of their past and their link to a father who had been executed. Mariia lived alone, in great need. Her relatives helped her as much as they could.

The remaining sisters lived a short distance from one another. Their mother was delighted, anticipating a long-awaited meeting with all her children and grandchildren. Love and intimacy were abundant in this large family.

We quickly fulfilled his mother's wish and visited his father's grave. The next day we called on Anton's cousins. These families also experienced unbelievable difficulties. The head of one household had been arrested and condemned to an unknown fate. In another family, a son had been killed by a tractor while he was working in the field. The poverty in their huts was visible everywhere.

Seeing all of this suffering, my thoughts kept returning me to my own past. I asked myself: why think of the past? I was happy and had a husband who loved me. Yet fear followed me everywhere like a dark cloud overhead. There were times when I was happy in the company of others and suddenly, in an instant, I would stiffen with fear. It sometimes seemed to me that it was sinful to be happy, knowing how many unfortunate people surrounded us.

On the third day of our visit, Anton, his sister Vanda, and I headed for a neighboring village, with the hope of buying a piglet to roast for our wedding dinner. We wandered all day from one small wooden hut of the collective farms to the next. What pitiful lives we observed! In one hut, children were sitting on the floor around a cast-iron pot of potato soup, which was blue from the reaction of the liquid with the metal. The children ate this soup with wooden spoons. We asked where their mother was.

"In the field," answered the eldest boy, confirming

our hunch that we need not bother asking whether they had a piglet. Filth was everywhere. The fleas attacked us like mosquitoes. My legs were covered with red spots.

We had to go three kilometers more to another village. Here we immediately noticed a difference. There were trees around the huts and flowers beneath the windows. We were lucky at the very first house. The owner, an old woman, said that she had three piglets and that she could sell the largest one so she could buy soap, sugar, and perhaps calico for a dress for her daughter, who worked in the collective farm office. We settled on a price, caught the piglet, and put him into a sack. Anton threw the sack over his shoulder; the piglet struggled and squealed.

"Vanda, why is this village so much more clean and pleasant than the first?" I asked.

"Catholics live in this village, and in the first . . ." She stopped short; she didn't want to say "Orthodox," for fear of offending me.

I thought about this. After all, the Orthodox toiled just the same. What was the matter? My answer to myself was that because there was little work and due to their poverty our people were bitter and tried to distance themselves from one another. Living in such primitive conditions gave rise to malice and envy. The Catholics were in the minority, and they understood that if they weren't united they wouldn't exist at all. They would disappear in the stormy torrent in the struggle for existence under the Soviet system.

I became still sadder and more pained for our people. It was terrible to live in such a rich country and to see such poverty and need only because there was no order in it, no faith or love for one another. Who established such conditions for our breadwinners?

These thoughts merely supplemented observations I made while working my first year in a rural district. In fulfilling my duties, I had to visit my pupils' homes to inspect the everyday conditions of their lives. Of course, in my reports I could not state the true conditions of people's lives. I could only refer to incidents of physical assaults on children or the parents' drunkenness and violence. I could not mention the real conditions of life, which had been created by the Soviet system.

It was in this dark mood that I accompanied my husband and sister-in-law home. They talked about their other relatives whom I had not yet met.

"Why are you silent, Lenok?" Anton asked me.

"I'm thinking. I'm always thinking."

"About what?"

"About the complexity of life."

"Are you taking up philosophy?"

"No, only everyday reality," I answered. Then there was a prolonged silence, which I broke.

"You know, I am happy that we have bought the piglet, but on the other hand I pity him. To kill an animal, in order to make merry!"

"Well, Lenochka, everything in nature is arranged thus. Yes, a man kills animals in order to feed himself, and this is justified. Why are there people who, much worse than beasts, kill people? For what? Who can justify that?" said Anton.

We changed the topic of conversation to avoid further arguments. Vanda began to tell of her family and even touched on the infidelity of her husband, whom she still loved very much.

Of all the sisters, Vanda was the least beautiful in appearance, but with an immeasurable kindness. In her I saw a person who could be an example to many. She spoke in a quiet, calm voice, avoided any condemnation of others, and helped all her relatives and acquaintances. She loved her mother dearly. In her kindness and generosity, she reminded me of my own mother. When she spoke with me, she looked intently into my eyes, as if trying to read my thoughts.

Within a week, all the relatives had arrived. It was very noisy and cheerful in the house, but I felt somewhat lonely, since there was not a single soul from my side of the family.

The celebratory dinner went superbly. There were many different foods and drinks. They constantly cried *gor'ko!*[3] Neither Anton nor I objected: we fulfilled their demand and kissed each other. The relatives expressed aloud their opinion that they were fully in agreement with Anton's choice of a wife. I don't know whether this was sincere or not. I only know that Anton's mother and Vanda, with whom I had already spent an entire week, had grown fond of me. Time passed quickly, and soon we had to return home.

Tears and laughter mingled on the day of our departure. Anton was proud of the fact that his family liked me. Regardless of the success of the visit, I felt a heaviness in my soul. Indeed, there are such serious moments when a person has a premonition of catastrophe. No matter how one tries to drive away these thoughts, they nevertheless pursue relentlessly.

On the way home we again stopped at Viktoriia's in Minsk. Near a large first-class store downtown, we unexpectedly met my husband's friend Evgenii and his wife. We were all astonished by such an unexpected encounter. Addressing Anton, Evgenii asked, "Antok, how did this happen? You and Lena?"

"Yes, she is my wife," answered Anton.

"I can't believe it! When did you meet each other?" continued Evgenii, completely forgetting that he had not introduced his companion to us. "Oh, yes! This is my wife Valentina." The woman blushed and extended her hand to us. Valentina was a doctor of medicine, quite plump, but with an intelligent face. The four of us dropped into a cafe, had some tea, and parted.

I began to pity Anya, who had loved Evgenii so much. Already another woman had taken her place. I wondered what had happened to her and whether she knew of Evgenii's marriage.

The next day we were on the train at six o'clock in the morning, and the mournful whistles of the steam engines carried me away again to the past. Two emotions churned inside me: a feeling of joy that we were going home to pursue our goal of building our life and a feeling of uncertainty and fear, not unlike that when my family had been forced from our home. I tried to think about pleasant things. With me traveled a dear, beloved man, all of whose attention was concentrated on diverting me from my sorrowful memories. He had promised to look after me, to love and to help me in everything, and never to leave me.

We were on the road for almost an entire day. Since we rode in the sleeping car, we were not tired at all. We ate in the dining car where the food was mediocre but expensive. Many passengers sat too long at the little tables and drank glass after glass of vodka. I was happy that my husband did not drink and did not smoke. One cannot say that his eyes didn't follow beautiful women, who also glanced his way. While some Russian men believed that a man who didn't drink, smoke, and chase after women was not really a man at all, I knew that my husband was a real man, loving his people and his homeland.

I was truly happy with him. At times I felt like rising up and flying, embracing the whole world and shouting, "Thank you, thank you for the fact that I'm alive, that I have the ability to love others. Thank you for the gift of the Lord Most High, that fate has brought me together with a man who is so devoted to me and to whom I am so devoted. He is full of kindness and fairness."

Filled with anticipation of what joy our lives stretching ahead together might bring, we arrived back home and prepared for the beginning of a new school term.

4

Anton and I began preparing for the school year as soon as we returned from our trip. There were only two Russian schools in the city (the remainder were Byelorussian). My husband worked in one of them, and I ended up in the other. Officers, doctors, and other representatives of the Soviet elite sent their children to the Russian schools, because the majority of them were not Byelorussian.

My first task was to meet with the director of the school that Anatolii Sharralo had recommended. Anatolii had prepared me to some degree for this meeting. I knew that the director, a Party member, was a very strict woman. She was an old maid who was devoted to her work. Arriving at the school, a little nervous, I asked the secretary-typist where the director's office was. I went up to the second floor and knocked at the door.

"Yes, come in," said a somewhat hoarse voice. I entered and greeted her.

"Please sit down," she said, hardly looking at me. I extended to her the envelope from Anatolii.

"Your first name, patronymic, and surname," said Bronislava Iosifovna dryly.

I identified myself.

"How long have you been teaching?"

"One year."

"Where have you worked before?"

I named the two schools where I had worked.

After informing me of the policies in her school, Bronislava Iosifovna took me to the academic vice-president's office. She was also a woman of about fifty, but was very elegant and warm. We introduced ourselves. She gave me a schedule of classes, emphasizing that by the first teachers' meeting at the beginning of the first quarter all teachers should have prepared work plans for the entire year. The teachers worked six days a week.

"Nothing new," I thought.

I did not have a positive impression of the director, who seemed to me a persnickety bureaucrat. I had no choice but to work and try to fulfill what was expected of me. The first of these duties was the development of lesson plans for the year for each subject. I finished this task within several days. Although lessons hadn't yet started, my husband was already working entire days at school, and in the evenings he had to attend various meetings as the inspector of schools of the city district. I busied myself with domestic duties, even though I was a poor and impractical housekeeper.

Mother had always barred us children from the kitchen for some reason, allowing us only to help her clean the house. When Mother was away and my brother and sister had to polish the parquet floors, they soon discovered a convenient and quick method to make their work easier. After applying the wax, they forced me to sit on a sheepskin and dragged me about the floor by the legs. Of course, I screamed and thrashed, but there was no way out of my serving as an unwilling floor buffer. They were stronger than me and there were two of them against one of me. I still put up a fight every time.

Being stripped of our possessions and domestic comforts in Siberia, however, was the main reason for my lack of preparation for domestic chores. I will never forget the first time I cooked pearl-barley soup with pork.

One day I decided to treat my husband to his favorite lunch. I knew that he liked various soups and borshch and that he adored pearl-barley soup with pork most of all. I set the table beautifully and bought a small bouquet of flowers. Deciding that the soup had already boiled sufficiently, I turned off the stove.

Anton arrived. He sat at the table, and I proudly served his soup. Having swallowed a few spoonfuls, he suddenly said to me that he wasn't hungry and asked what was next. I was surprised. Only a year later did he tell me that the pearl-barley had been completely uncooked and hard. We both often laughed afterward, as we recalled my first culinary attempts.

A cleaning woman at Anton's school, named Lett, lived with her seventeen-year-old unemployed son in a small room in a garret. Her husband was a political prisoner. She washed our clothes, and I helped her with money. She saw my helplessness and tried to help me with the housekeeping.

The school year began. We both plunged into our work and were together only in the evenings, and sometimes not even then. On our days off, we tried to go to the theater or the cinema. I always carried my students' homework with me since I had to draft a complete summary of the lessons each day without fail. We would go to sleep very late and get up at 6:30 A.M. To get to my school, I walked from our apartment to the main street, caught a tram, and arrived fifteen to twenty minutes later.

One night I worked until two o'clock and, being so sleepy, forgot to wind the alarm clock. The next morning I awoke and to my horror saw that it was 8:30, exactly the time my first class started. I began to cry loudly. Being late for work meant prison for certain! Anton leapt out of bed and began to run around in an effort to calm me. He grabbed my woolen *sarafan*,[4] slipped it over my flannel nightgown, then put my overcoat and hat on me. I snatched my briefcase and sprinted down the flights of stairs, three steps at a time, and raced breathlessly along the street.

I had to go down several more steps to get from our street to the main boulevard. The steps were covered with ice, and I slipped and nearly fell. Someone grabbed me from behind. He was a pilot and only said to me with a smile, "It's dangerous to fall like that."

I didn't even notice that my nightgown was sweeping the street. None of the passersby was surprised or dared laugh, since everyone knew what the consequences of being late to work could be. ("It has become better to live, gayer to live, comrades!")

It was senseless to wait for the tram, and I ran the whole way up the steep hill to the school. Reaching the school, I raced up the stairs to the staff room and suddenly dropped to the floor, my face a mask of red and white patches. Only one woman, a Young Pioneer leader, was in the office at this time. She took one look and quickly dashed away for the director of the school. Evidently, my appearance and dress—nightgown, shoes on bare feet, uncombed hair—had frightened her terribly. When she returned with the director, I had managed to catch my breath and could answer questions. They both helped me to my feet.

Bronislava Iosifovna invited me to come to her office. She sat me on a divan and gave me water. Fearing the consequences of my situation, I began to cry. The director tried to calm me, then went to her desk and called my husband to bring me proper clothing. "You can't go to class looking like that," she said.

Bronsilava Iosifovna sat close to me and said quietly that Elena Semeonovna, who was the academic vice-president, would take my place. "Don't worry, I won't submit a report on you," she continued. "You are a valuable teacher, the pupils love you, and I love your devotion to the job."

She added only one condition: that I not tell any of the other teachers. I continued to cry while listening to her.

It was reassuring to hear her comments about my work, since all the teachers knew how stern and demanding she was.

My husband appeared shortly after, and they both even exchanged jokes. "Apparently the honeymoon continues," noted Bronislava Iosifovna.

Anton blushed. "This wife of mine is a great worker and works day and night," he said as if trying to defend what had happened. He was right: I was loaded to the limit with work and had too little time for rest.

By the time I changed and made myself presentable, it was already the beginning of the third class. In the middle of the lesson, while I was writing on the chalkboard, all the pupils in my class suddenly arose. The director had entered and inquired how I was feeling. She left when I told her I was fine, but my pupils looked questioningly at me. My face was still covered with red spots, and I must have appeared very distracted.

When lessons were finished, the teachers were supposed to remain in the staff room until five o'clock or give special attention to lagging students. As soon as I sat down at the table in the teachers' room that day, Bronislava Iosifovna entered and quietly said to me, "Go home, lie down and rest. This is not advice, but an order."

"I have a lot of work. I will not be able to return the homework notebooks to the pupils tomorrow."

"That's all right. Catch up on your day off."

I obeyed and headed home.

The next day was Saturday, and I was already at work earlier than usual. All the teachers were there except for one, Vera Ivanova. Married to the captain of an infantry unit, she could obtain things at reduced prices in closed stores. She was better dressed than all of us and even had a fur coat made from seals.

Only ten minutes remained until the bell when she burst into the teachers' room and hastily took off her fur coat. We didn't dare laugh and did not know whether we should tell her to keep her coat on. Seeing our frozen faces, she looked at herself from top to bottom and discovered to her deep embarrassment that she was wearing only a blouse and no slip and that we could see the garters for her stockings.

With a shriek, she quickly threw on her coat. Her eyes filled with tears, and her face turned crimson. She was horribly ashamed. I got up from the table and went to her.

"Vera Ivanovna, there is not and cannot be disgrace of any kind here. We all understand . . . it is clear that you hurried so as not to be late for work."

"Yes, yes!" she said guiltily. "What shall I do now?"

"Go to class in the fur coat. There is nothing wrong with that," I advised her.

Not only teachers but all those who worked found themselves in similar circumstances. On the tram, I often saw a man who worked in a textile factory. One day he was late for work, so he knocked out a window of the tram with his elbow. The conductor stopped the tram at an intersection where a militiaman was standing. The worker was arrested and taken to the local militia office. He had to pay a fine, of course, but at the same time he received a note that he had been detained by the police. This note served as an official excuse to the factory administration. Better to break the law and pay a fine than be sent to prison for the simple infraction of being late. Adapting to the situation, workers sometimes provoked artificial fights among themselves, after which arrests with fines would follow.

Usually all the seats of the slow-moving tram were occupied, and people stood crammed together in the aisles. When I entered the car, however, dozens of hands often shot up in the air.

"Elena Georgievna, Elena Georgievna! Sit in my place," cried my pupils. I usually sat in the nearest seat. It pleased me that my pupils were so courteous and that the majority of them would yield their seats to older people. Besides my students, the same passengers rode the tram each day. All of them, including the conductor, knew my name. Many passengers would always greet me with a smile, "Good morning, Elena Georgievna!"

I was very happy with my job at the school. I had up to 250 students each quarter and loved them all. Of course, this meant much work, but the results took away any fatigue. The pay for teachers was pitiful. A saleswoman at a bread shop earned more than a teacher. On the other hand, every person has his or her calling and sense of obligation to society.

Since my husband and I worked in different school districts, our periodic teachers' conferences were held at different times and places. It was frightening to walk along several out-of-the-way streets in the evening shadows. Thieves often stripped pedestrians and even killed them. One such incident happened to an acquaintance of mine. Returning home on a dark street after a meeting, she encountered a man who came up to her and very politely asked, "Tell me, please, is there a militiaman anywhere hereabouts?"

"No, I haven't seen one," she answered.

"Take off your coat quickly," ordered the thief, in the same polite tone. Fortunately, a worse fate didn't come to pass.

Fearing that something like that would happen to me, my husband usually arrived toward the end of our conferences and accompanied me home.

At one teachers' conference, we discussed improving instructional methods and attendance at so-called open lessons. During the meeting, the names of the school district's best teachers were called, and mine was among them. Sitting next to me, my husband looked at me with a proud smile.

"And you didn't want me in your school, fearing that you would be ashamed of me if I turned out to be a bad teacher," I thought to myself. "You were mistaken," my thoughts mocked reproachfully. But I never asked him to explain why he did not tell me about the opening in his school.

Anton was a demanding teacher, but he was also demanding of himself. When he began as academic vice-president at the school, discipline among the students was terrible. There were times when the students threw school benches out the windows into the street. They were also generally rude to the teachers. The director of the school, a very nice and mild Jewish man, was not a Party member. Anton and he became friends and discussed methods to improve the situation at the school. Ninety-five percent of the students in this Russian school were the children of the more privileged families, and it was therefore difficult to contend with them.

When a history teacher named Tumanova, who was a member of the Communist Party, appeared on the scene, their work began to be undermined. She wanted to be named director. It was intolerable to her that neither the director nor the academic vice-president was a Party member.

"How can non-Party teachers educate children in the Communist spirit?" she asked once at a teachers' meeting. No one dared to answer her question. This was indeed extremism, since all the textbooks and lectures were full of this poison. Nobody could dare be objective in teaching.

One day a representative of the local district Party committee visited my literature class. He was an ignoramus in both appearance and speech. I read Pushkin's poem "Poltava" to the class. Since this is a historical poem, what element of Communist education could be introduced while analyzing it? At the end of the lesson, the representative wrote the following in clumsy handwriting in my daily lesson plan: "The lesson was conducted very well. But it is necessary to point out that the instructress did not make the transition, the bridge from Peter the First to the present day. She did not underscore the importance of the education of the young in the Communist spirit."

I saw that he talked with the director of the school after the lesson, but she had always been on my side. When I got home that day and showed this rebuke to my husband, he advised me to be more careful in the future. Indeed, Anton had to be careful, too, because Tumanova could undermine him, especially if she felt that he displayed no amorous feelings toward her. After all, her denunciation to the NKVD would be weighty, and no one would be able to dispute it. This troubled me greatly.

Toward the end of the last school quarter of 1941, I was expecting a child, and Anton told me that I should transfer to his school. Even though my earlier life had been one of repeated uprootings, I never liked moving from one place to another or changing my place of work, especially now, when my relationship was excellent with both the administration and my students. Anton began to insist urgently, but Bronislava Iosifovna did not even want to listen to him.

The school year ended, and all that needed to be done

was finished. I was tired and strained. The experience in Siberia continued to affect my health, particularly in my pregnant condition. My feet and eyes swelled, which worried Anton. He began to ask me to go to his mother's place without him. I objected. Although I already liked his relatives, I didn't want to go without him. Who can take the place of a husband? Anton was still very busy at work and could not get leave for another three weeks.

At this time we also began to apply for a larger and more comfortable communal apartment. Because the mother of one of my students was the head of the Department of Housing, we learned that there was a house with four apartments in a very beautiful place on the banks of the river Dvina. One apartment was vacant, as the head of the family had been transferred to a position in another city.

One of the requirements for securing this apartment was that there had to be two or three children in the family, but, of course, we were expecting only our first child. Influence has its privileges, however, and the head of the department simply wrote that we had two children. Thus functioned the machinery of the Soviet bureaucracy.

We were delighted with our new apartment. There was only one bath and lavatory in the house and a communal kitchen, and the tenants shared cleaning duties. Having such facilities was considered a luxury because now it wasn't necessary to go outside to the lavatory.

Anton came home for lunch and repeatedly raised the question of my departure. "They are waiting for you there and will be happy to see you," he would say. "And you will get rest." Usually I was silent, but finally I had to agree with my husband and prepared to leave without him. We had lived in the new apartment for only seven days.

I began writing a letter to my mother and sister, letting them know that I would be going to Anton's family's place. I wrote them of my joy that my mother had surprised us earlier with an unexpected visit. She had explained her visit by saying that, since she did not have long to live, she wanted once more to see me and, in particular, her son-in-law before her death. She liked Anton very much and blessed us both. This was the last time that we saw her. In the letter I urged her to take care of herself and said that I wanted her to visit us again after her grandchild was born. I understood the risks connected with her trip. After all, she had no passport, and they might arrest her at the very first check, regardless of the fact that she was a complete invalid.

In preparation for the journey, I went to the drugstore and decided along the way to stop by the school where my husband worked. I went up to the second floor. It was quiet, because the students were already on vacation. I opened the door to Anton's office. He was sitting at his desk.

Tumanova was standing next to him, leaning on his shoulder. Anton reddened, and she quickly pulled her hand from his shoulder and straightened up.

"We are examining a few problems here," he tried to explain to me, speaking quickly. Tumanova was silent, with an expression of arrogance, perhaps insolence on her face.

"Excuse me for disturbing you. I will see you at home," I said and turned toward the exit. Anton jumped up from his seat and hurried after me.

"Did you want to say something to me?"

"No," I answered. "I dropped in because I was nearby and just wanted to say hello to you." I headed for the stairway without turning my head. I had never been jealous by nature. Now something sank in my heart, and I returned home pensive.

I knew that many unmarried and divorced women had tried to attract Anton's attention when he had been a bachelor and that very beautiful female teachers had been among his admirers. Tumanova had immediately disliked me since our first meeting at a reception in her apartment. The reason was Anton.

Tumanova was married to the *politruk* of a regiment, which meant that she could dress with great taste. She was not beautiful, but she was elegant. A member of the Communist Party, she had been graduated in history and believed herself at the pinnacle of her profession. She was quite bold and betrayed her husband at every opportunity, since he was often away and she saw him very rarely.

Anton came home early that day. Coming into the apartment, he saw me sitting at the table continuing the letter to my mother and my sister. He walked over to me, touched my shoulder, and kissed my cheek. I began writing again, so I could finish the letter and send it before my departure. Sealing the envelope, I asked my husband if he would like to eat.

"No, only a glass of tea," he answered. "I don't want you to fix anything."

"It's no bother for me. What would you like for supper?" I always tried to prepare his favorite dishes, although it wasn't always possible to purchase the necessary food. My homemaking skills were still poor, but improving.

"Lenusenka, you aren't angry with me?"

"For what? Why should I be angry?"

"Because that impudent woman was hanging on my neck."

"That's her problem, not mine, and I hope not yours."

"I was afraid it upset you when you saw her on my shoulder."

"Do you think that I should be upset? Is there any basis for this?"

"No, of course, no! After all, you know that I love only you, and may you never have thoughts that I could betray you."

Notwithstanding his persuasion, heavy thoughts wandered through my head. I wanted to believe him, that he sincerely loved only me. I especially did not want to leave home without him now, but the day of my departure came. I had packed only a small suitcase, since Anton planned to bring with him anything else we needed. It was easier for me to travel without a lot of baggage. My husband was especially tender and attentive to me on the day of my departure, and I felt these gestures were sincere.

We arrived at the terminal with time to spare before the train's eleven o'clock departure, so we stopped by the buffet and had a lemonade. I had obtained my berth in the sleeping car through connections. I got in the car. Anton didn't go away from the window but stood on the platform. I begged him to come as soon as he could, and he promised. The train started to move away and gather speed. Suddenly,

I wanted to leap from the car and to run back to my husband. I wasn't thinking of the incident in his office, but of something inexplicable. I had an overwhelming sense of bad tidings to come, almost as if the whistles of the locomotive were singing to me in harmony with my thoughts: "Farewell! Farewell!"

The conductor brought the bedding. When I tried to rest I only tossed and turned and couldn't fall asleep. I don't remember what time the train arrived at Orsha. Our sleeping car was uncoupled and left on a siding. I arose from the bed and opened the window. The air smelled of smoke. Dawn was breaking. I was deeply absorbed in painful reflections, and a horrible anguish lacerated my soul.

"What if I never see him again and am again left alone and defenseless in some great grief?" I asked myself.

"But how stupid you are!" my voice answered. "Why would I not see him? After all, he loves me and is such a decent man! He hopes that a son will be born to us. No, no! Nothing can happen to separate us from each other," I convinced myself. My thoughts alternated from one outlook to the other. For the most part, however, they were not joyful.

In deep thought at the open window, I didn't take note of a freight train of at least seventy cars chugging by. Then I saw faces behind the gratings of the small windows, almost beneath the roofs of the cars. Prisoners! I then noticed the armed guard in the distance, which confirmed my suspicion.

"Where are you from?" I asked one prisoner quietly.

"We are from the Pribaltic states. They're taking us somewhere, but we don't know where. What city is this?"

"Orsha," I answered. I saw only men's faces in the car, which meant the families would follow later. Images of my past experiences, living in my soul just beneath the surface, flashed before my eyes. As I thought about my family's misfortunes, I began to pity these people. How many of them would perish from hunger, cold, and diseases?

Sympathy for these sufferers further added to my foreboding of something terrible. Why had they arrested these people? What had they done against society? Probably their only fault was that they were born into this period in history. Like millions of our people, they were not guilty of a crime. Yet fathers were torn from their children, husbands from their wives, sons from their mothers and fathers! Where was justice? Truth? The law? The prisoners' fear and silence attested to the lack of convincing answers to these questions.

Wave after wave of arrests had swept the country during the 1930s. I remember one time when they were arresting even peasants during a period when Trotskyites[5] were being rounded up and arrested. During an interrogation, an agent forced a peasant woman to sign a confession that she was a Trotskyite and a member of the "conspiracy" to overthrow Stalin. The peasant woman implored him to believe her denial, but he would not.

"My little son, I have never even stood near a tractor. What could I have done to it?"

That was how she understood the word "Trotskyite."

I remember another incident, when a neighbor of ours received an American dollar inserted into a letter from the United States. The authorities considered any connection with foreigners a crime, and of course this letter had been opened and the neighbor arrested. During the interrogation, the officer severely beat him and demanded a confession to the "spy activity" for which he had received the money.

The government ordered the general population to redeem all gold and silver. Everyone tried to hide gold currency or jewelry articles as irreplaceable memories of the past. Someone informed on one peasant, claiming that he had hidden several five-ruble gold pieces. Special agents went to the peasant's home and arrested him. The man confessed during the interrogation that the coins were hidden in a red rag behind the lintel of the door. Secret agents from the criminal investigation department went to his house and found the coins. They were not in a red rag, however, but in a blue one. The officers then beat him again so he would tell them where the gold coins in the red rag were located. There weren't any, of course; the man had confused the colors in his fright. The authorities continued their torture and then finally released him. The unfortunate man somehow reached his own bathhouse on the bank of a small river, where he died in the entrance hall.

No one raised a voice of protest at such atrocities. So repressed were our people that they simply accepted the hardships and didn't even dare think about the morality of the government's actions. This was due not to cowardice but to fear for loved ones. There was no mercy for anyone who was labeled an enemy of the people, a spy, or a saboteur.

The government was packed with officials who at one time had nothing, but then had become all-powerful under the Stalinist regime. These were people who tried to destroy everything and annihilate all those who labored, made gains, or helped others. Of course, it is not fair to generalize that all the poor were evil avengers or, on the other hand, that there were no cruel or greedy exploiters among the prosperous.

Nevertheless, government officials and representatives must have possessed the psyches of murderers to kill all the innocent people so pitilessly or to fling young children through train windows to die in the snow during the hardest frosts. Let no one doubt the truthfulness of these incidents. I saw them myself and heard the crying of the children and mothers and the quiet moans of the fathers.

5

Witnessing the dismal plight of the prisoners and brooding over my dark premonitions made my heart heavy as I arrived in Minsk. I tried to think of a future more happy than my past, but sad memories pushed aside my dreams.

At the terminal I found my husband's sister Viktoriia and her eldest daughter waiting for me. It was nine o'clock in the morning. They were glad to see me, though they were disappointed that Anton had not come with me. We set off for their apartment. I didn't feel entirely well. My feet were swollen, so I could not put on shoes and had to wear slippers. I had bags under my eyes.

As soon as we entered the apartment, Viktoriia suggested we eat breakfast. I declined, since I wanted to go to bed. My whole body was shaking, from fatigue, from my tormenting thoughts, or from the foreboding of some inevitable catastrophe. It felt as though I had parted from my husband forever.

For a long time I was not able to fall asleep, but I finally dozed off. In a dream I saw Anton, dressed in a dark suit. He wanted to write something, but was unable to. I cried for some reason, and he tried to comfort me. I was awakened by what I thought was Viktoriia's sobbing. The door to my room was slightly ajar, and through the opening I saw her raise her hands and say something. I listened a while and saw that she was indeed crying.

"Viktoriia, what's happened?" I asked in alarm. She ran into the room and said in a trembling voice, "Lenochka! War! Hitler has attacked us!"

I quickly leapt from the bed. "This cannot be! What about the Nonaggression Pact?"

A siren blared in the city, signaling an air raid. Molotov's voice boomed over the loudspeaker: "Hitler has attacked us, but our cause is just; the enemy will be defeated. Victory will be ours."

"Viktoriia, I have to send a telegram to Anton right now, but I don't know where there's a telegraph. Let's go together."

We were ready in a flash and went out to the main street. Complete confusion reigned in the city. Near a public garden, we saw the first captured German paratroopers who had been dropped to the rear in Red Army uniforms. They had been beaten, and blood trickled down their faces. I felt faint at the sight of the blood. We learned Germans could easily be identified by their clean new uniforms and short boots. I managed to send the telegram, which I later learned Anton received and immediately answered. I never received his response, since communication of all kinds was cut.

Discussing the situation, Viktoriia and I decided that I should try to reach my mother-in-law's place; it would be quieter in the country. Chaos dominated the train terminal. Those who had been called to duty, and Red Army soldiers and commanders who had been on leave, were all trying to return to their units. Late in the evening I finally was able to get a seat and departed for the village where Anton's mother lived.

It was a terrible and eerie night. There were no lights anywhere. Most of the people on the train were silent, and when someone spoke, it was in a whisper. When we reached the station, I heard someone playing a concertina. Young people had gathered to see off the recruits in a small park next to the station.

"How can they play music and dance at such a time?" I wondered. But this merriment was with tears.

It was two kilometers from the station to my mother-in-law's house. I plodded along in the darkness. When I knocked at the door, my mother-in-law opened it and embraced me wordlessly and firmly. Only then did she ask, "What will happen to Anton? The poor dear, there won't even be anyone to see him off to the front."

"We'll be with him in our thoughts," I answered.

Her words were as painful as throwing salt on an open wound. The reasons for my bad omen when I left were now clear, and I realized why I had wanted to run from the train and not to leave him alone. What sorrow burdened my heart!

Anton's sister Vanda and her husband entered her mother's room. Heavy bombers already rumbled menacingly above us. None of us thought to go to sleep. We all sat fully dressed and awaited a terrible unknown something. The dawn finally peeped through the window.

The house was located far from the highway, but a back road ran beyond the garden and a small field. A stream of people on foot—both civilians and soldiers—moved along it. Everyone was frightened at the prospect and very word of war. Passersby, who came to the house to quench their thirst with cold water, kept asking where the Germans were.

The Germans followed on their heels. The next day I saw an air battle between Soviet and German fighter planes. There were three German and five Soviet airplanes. All of ours were shot down and fell to earth in fiery balls. This made me even more depressed. I even suggested to Anton's mother that we retreat with all the passing Red Army units.

"To where? And in your condition? Look at your feet,

at your belly! Can such people really retreat?" she angrily responded.

"But I don't want to be left with the enemy; God knows what they will do with us! Better to die on the road than from an enemy's bullet," I retorted.

My mother-in-law remembered the Germans from the First World War and tried to tell me of their conduct. I didn't even want to listen. "They are the enemy. They have attacked us. They are already bombing our cities!" I shouted.

Deep down, I myself knew that there was nowhere to run. Shattered units of the Soviet army passed by us in the first days of the war. How many others went by different roads or through the forests?

"My husband and brother are probably marching somewhere, too," I thought in despair. "Where are they? Perhaps already killed by the first enemy bombs or shells." Inconsolable grief tormented my heart. I began to fear the effects of my anxiety and insomnia on my pregnancy. Only my pregnancy kept me from complete breakdown, at least for a short time.

In the days following the invasion, more and more Soviet retreaters passed by the house, and more and more German airplanes flew in the skies. Bullets from these low-flying fighter craft rained down on the hapless Soviets, who would scatter in the fields or hide beneath trees or in huts and barns. Many Soviet soldiers were barefoot, their feet bloody and worn to calluses. Some continued to carry their weapons, but others walked without them.

Early one morning I walked to the station to find out what was going on in the world. Even though there was little hope of learning anything new, I dreamed that perhaps a telegram would arrive from Anton to his sister, whose husband worked at the station. No one was able to tell me anything definite besides what everyone already knew: that the Soviet army was retreating in disorder, that the first mortal blow had been dealt by the Germans to the concentration of the Soviet army on the Polish border, and that many bunkers had been blown up along with the people inside them. The enemy had caught us so unsuspecting that we even saw soldiers rushing out of their buildings wearing only their underwear.

Where was our Intelligence Service? What about the friendship of Stalin and Hitler? And what about Molotov and Ribbentrop?[6] All the retreaters asked themselves and each other these questions. There were rumors that even Marshal Kulik, a top commander, himself went on foot across our region. I met Uralova, the People's Commissar of Education in Byelorussia, walking barefoot, her feet covered with wounds. She asked for some cold water. Soldierless commanders often asked permission to stop at our barn for a little rest.

Household responsibilities fell on my shoulders. We baked bread from the last reserves of flour, cooked cabbage soup, and fed at least some of the retreaters (giving food to all of them would have been impossible). Some of the Red Army soldiers already had a few stalks of wheat or some crusts of bread in their mess tins. I pitied these people, who, after all, were our persecuted brothers. Of course, we were all victims.

Returning home from the station one day, I was walking behind a group of soldiers. One of them still had a rifle on his shoulder, and another had his boots thrown over his shoulder and was limping. One of his heels was bloody. I could hear fragments of their conversation. "I tell you, throw away the rifle, you fool!" the unarmed solder said to the other. "After all, Voroshilov said that we will beat the enemy on his own territory.[7] And you want to fight on your own?"

"No, I won't throw it away!" the soldier answered. "The regrouping point is at Berezino, and I will carry it there."

"What is there to fight for? For the fact that my father died in a concentration camp? For the fact that my entire family was destroyed in the purges?"

Such sorrow and sarcasm! Many felt similar sentiments. Red Army soldiers fell prisoner to the enemy by the thousands, and the invasion continued still farther across our borders. The best military commanders had been destroyed in Stalin's purges throughout the 1930s, leaving the army in complete disorganization and unpreparedness. "We will beat the enemy on his own territory" was a battle cry.

The Soviet people would sing songs:

> Beloved city, you may sleep peacefully
> And dream and grow green in spring.

In reality, those first units of the Red Army and the towns and cities they tried to defend became the first victims of the invasion.

The German Air Force mercilessly hunted and killed our retreating soldiers. During one such attack, their airplanes made a run over our house and raked it with machine gun fire. When it had quieted a little, I crawled out of the cellar and heard the heartrending moans of the injured and dying. I took some bed sheets from my mother-in-law's trunk and cut them into bandages to provide first aid in the field. Some of the wounded had both legs broken by bullets, and others had open abdominal cavities. I wiped off the blood, dressed the wounds, dragged the soldiers into the shade of the trees, placed wet rags on their heads, and gave them some water to swallow. Making these rounds, I forgot that the sight of blood had once made me feel faint or that seeing the suffering and the dead made me feel squeamish.

"Where are you, my dear brother?" I thought. "You see, I haven't died, seeing death. I am helping them, and I hope that perhaps someone will give the same aid to you and to my husband."

My sister-in-law Vanda was my faithful assistant, but she was afraid to touch the wounded. She could only cut up the linen, make bandages, and bring hot and cold water. My mother-in-law boiled water for washing out the wounds. The neighbors followed our example and, in difficult cases, sent for me as a "doctor." Thus a first-aid station was organized, although without a sanitary atmosphere or proper equipment.

After we rendered first aid, many were able to continue their retreat. Some others had to recover while resting on hay beds in the barns. Many of them never recovered but went on to the other world. I could not even imagine sleep during those days, even though I had no strength to move.

My legs were swollen up to the knees, and I struggled around barefoot.

Early one morning I went out and made the rounds of my patients and afterward lay down beneath an apple tree and dozed off. Feeling the touch of someone's hand, I opened my eyes. My mother-in-law was standing before me.

"Get up, Lena. The Germans have come."

I began to tremble with fear. In the first days of the invasion, the radio broadcast stories saying that when the Germans occupied a territory they cut open the stomachs and cut off the breasts of pregnant women.

"But why are you calling me?" I said, annoyed.

"Well, you speak German," Anton's mother said guiltily.

I got up and went to the house. Two strapping Germans were sitting on the porch. They both got up when I approached, we exchanged greetings, and they asked me if I understood German.

"Yes, a little," I answered quietly.

"What is the name of this village?" asked one.

I gave the name. They explained to me that they had gotten lost from their parachute unit and that their assembly point was the village of Dukora. They unrolled a map, and I showed them the direction with a trembling hand. After all, we didn't have road signs anywhere. The second German, who had been silent at first, noted how I was trembling all over. He asked me why I trembled so. I didn't answer, and he said with a smile, "Don't be afraid, we won't do anything to you."

They thanked me and left, but I still shook for a long time and couldn't get hold of myself. This was my first meeting with the Germans, but it was not my last. A few days later, whole units of the German armed forces passed through our area. The Soviet troops were scattered; a few formations still hid in the forests. The retreat was shameful and disorganized. The wounded Red Army soldiers who weren't able to go on had to change clothes to hide the fact that they were soldiers.

My in-laws had a dog named Zhuchok that was my husband's favorite. One time a German soldier entered the yard and headed toward the doghouse, apparently ready to kill it. I ran out of the house and stood in front of the dog. It evidently helped that I spoke German and was able to explain that Zhuchok was always on a chain and didn't run about the streets.

During the retreat, many Red Army soldiers hid in villages or forests and became common-law husbands of women who were alone or disabled. These women considered themselves fortunate. Such young couples worked in the fields and repaired dilapidated huts. The collective farms were broken up, and the peasants worked for themselves. Of course, they had to give food to the Germans.

Hitler depended on a blitzkrieg to end the war quickly, but this tactic did not work as planned. Although the first shock units raced deeply into the country and the German army was excellently supplied and trained, their forces were stretched thinly in a vast foreign land. The transportation network was not equal to the task, so supplying themselves with war materials grew more difficult.

The Germans used ploys to take huge numbers of prisoners. At first, German parachute units would feed their captives and then release them, saying, "Go home to Mommy." The retreating prisoners would then walk to the rear, meet new Soviet units, and share their experience as German prisoners. This deception helped the enemy capture more than a million surrendering Red Army soldiers and later cost thousands of prisoners their lives.

One former prisoner told us about the treatment accorded him in one of the countless camps. The Germans had fenced in a field with wire and driven the prisoners behind the wire—like livestock. The prisoners sat beneath the burning sun with nothing to eat or drink. After two weeks, when there were already many dead among them, the guards opened a narrow exit to a small stream. The prisoners, having become like animals concerned only with survival, threw themselves at the water. At that time bursts of machine gun fire resounded from all the machine gun towers. The prisoner, pretending to be dead, lay beneath a corpse and drank water mixed with human blood. Reports of similar incidents began to reach the Soviet army. Those who had escaped death told others, and the surrenders changed from thousands to only occasional individuals.

Living at my mother-in-law's and watching all that was happening around us, I suffered from great anxiety. Worry was my constant companion in my dreams and while awake. I feared that my child would not be born normal, because of such nervous tension and the burden of caring for the rest of the family. Indeed, I had to provide strength to my elderly mother-in-law and to Vanda and her husband, who was an incredible coward, afraid to show himself in the street. His cowardice was demonstrated many times.

For example, before the invasion, Vanda and her husband employed a Jewish shoemaker from Warsaw, who had fled his divided homeland with his wife. Now that the Germans were here, he could not escape, and he stayed with us. Since the Germans drove all the Jews into ghettos, we hid him in our cellar. The Germans often mounted searches, seeking weapons as well as people. We had to do something to save this man and ourselves as well, for if they found him with us, they would execute the entire family.

We decided to take him away to the forest, where many were already in hiding. Who should take this unfortunate man away? Vanda's husband categorically refused, afraid of being caught. I felt only shame for him. I was chosen, so we harnessed the horse, put straw in the cart, and concealed the shoemaker beneath it. I drove off with him toward Dukora.

At the time, many people already knew who I was. The Germans called me *Lehrerin*, teacher, and our own people knew me for the moral aid I gave them. No one stopped me during this journey. My hands trembled the entire time, and I wanted to convince myself that I felt no fear at all. Such self-deception! I was terrified.

I drove into the forest, looked around, and quietly instructed him to crawl out. Without saying a word, my poor passenger dragged himself into the depths of the forest and I returned home. Dusk fell, followed by the darkness of night. The weight of events developing all around—the humiliation, fear of the unknown, and the pain of separation from the people dear to me—tormented my heart. Oh, how I had always hated darkness!

Later that night I heard someone creeping up to our house and then a quiet knock at the door.

"Who's there?" I asked in alarm.

"It's me, open quickly!" I recognized my morning passenger's voice.

"Why have you returned? What happened?"

He was not able to answer my questions right away. He was trembling all over, and his teeth chattered. He said that he had sat in the marsh the whole day and, not finding a single living soul, decided to return. We could do nothing but dry out his clothing and consider our next move. Vanda's husband avoided him throughout this whole episode, even though it was he who had invited the shoemaker to come repair all of the family's shoes. He was fed and paid for his labor. It was not really my business, except I felt everyone has a duty to aid a fellow human being in danger.

It was already the second month of the war when I lay down to rest after lunch one August day. I wasn't able to fall asleep and listened to every sound. Suddenly I heard the gate in the yard creak, accompanied by quick steps.

"Lena, Lena! Aunt Evdokia!" Anton's cousin's wife cried. "Antok is coming, I recognized him in the distance! It's him! Quickly, come see! It's him! It's him!"

I heard all of this clearly, but could not understand whether it was a dream or if I was already delirious. I groggily leapt from the bed and, instead of heading toward the door, tried to climb out the window. When I finally found myself in the hallway, my mother-in-law, Vanda, Elena, and the children were already there.

When Elena said once again that she had recognized Anton walking toward us through the meadow, I don't know what happened. I revived when I caught the strong smell of liquid ammonia. Anton's mother had tried to open my mouth with a metal spoon, and to this day I have two chipped front teeth.

Opening my eyes, I saw my husband on his knees, bending over me. My aged mother-in-law was next to him and said to me in tears, "What's wrong with you? Your husband comes, and you, how do you greet him?"

Anton caressed my face with his hand and said in a quiet voice, "I'm home, my darling. I am with you!" It seemed like a joyful dream. I could not believe that my husband was here standing before me. For his part, Anton had not known whether I had reached his mother's or had been killed in Minsk during the bombing.

They helped me to get up and sit on a bench. Looking at his emaciated figure, I noticed that one of his feet was wrapped in a blood-soaked rag.

"You are wounded!" I cried.

"No, Lenochka, I blistered my feet with my shoes. After all, I've crossed five hundred kilometers on foot."

When I unrolled the rag, I saw that the entire sole of his foot was a continuous festering wound. As home doctor, I immediately set about my duty. We obtained some of the medical supplies necessary to disinfect his wound through the local apothecary.

"How were you able to walk?" I asked. "The pain must be unbearable."

"I didn't think of the pain, didn't think of the war and death," he replied. "I only walked with the thought of seeing you more quickly."

The house where we had moved seven days before my departure had been destroyed by a shell, and all of our humble belongings were lost. Anton said the whole house rose into the air and fell like a pancake. Thank God that at that time he was at his school. Most important, both our lives were spared, and we were together now. This was a miracle!

When the mobilization had begun on the first day of the war, Anton had to appear at the draft office and was assigned to a unit of infantrymen. None of these mobilized units was able to go anywhere, since uninterrupted bombings and artillery fire had begun.

The Germans already occupied much territory when Anton left the city on foot. The Germans detained Anton along the way, as they did with many of the wandering men. His hair, cut very short in preparation for military service, was proof to the Germans that he was a soldier. Anton's dark hair also made the Germans suspect he was a Jew, and in order to prove the opposite they forced him to unbutton his trousers.

All the detainees were gathered in an open-air camp, surrounded by guards, on the edge of a forest. No one was let out of it. Anton fortunately found himself at the forest itself. Although it wasn't so warm at first, it was easier to hide. One member of the camp's guard, a German soldier of Polish descent, aided Anton's escape from this camp. The guard somehow learned that Anton was Catholic and spoke Polish. One evening the soldier whispered to Anton, "Run!" and so he did, making his way through the forest and then along a back road for more than a month.

When Anton arrived, he was wearing his gray suit and had a small sack with clothing and dry pieces of bread over his shoulder. His lips trembled, for physical and spiritual exhaustion made it difficult for him even to speak. Through his tears, however, his eyes shone with joy. He was relieved to see that his whole family was alive.

"It's strange that when I tried to reach here as quickly as possible, I felt no fatigue," he said. "There were moments when I almost ran, but now it's hard for me to take even one step!"

"My dear, when a man strives toward some goal, his strength is inexhaustible. You knew that we were all absorbed with thoughts of you," I said. "Oh, Almighty Lord," I continued, not looking at my husband, "you heard my prayers and returned my husband to me!"

After shaving and washing, he was immediately transformed, and only his deeply sunken eyes spoke of his excessive weariness. His mother bustled about the kitchen, setting the table and preparing a meal for the hungry traveler. During dinner Anton said that on the way home he had thought about stopping at Orsha, where one of his sisters lived. She had grown sons who had obviously been mobilized. His desire to reach home as soon as possible had changed his plan. Now we were together, and we weren't troubled by the thought that all of our things had been lost. We were alive and awaiting an addition to the family. That was all that mattered.

The war raged all around us. Many of the Soviet prisoners who were spared from death were transported to Germany for hard labor. In the autumn following the invasion, they transferred the remaining prisoners from open fields to barracks. Typhus and other infectious diseases had begun to rage through the camps. The German command found a simple way to eliminate such epidemics. They drenched the barracks with gasoline and incinerated the infected and healthy prisoners alike.

The Germans were total masters of the occupied land. Hitler's army was brutal not only to the war prisoners, but to the entire nation. *Untermenschen*—inferior people—they called us. They believed that Russia was "a heap of dung" that needed only to be spread. However, when they tried to spread this heap, it began to smell strongly. Why? Because the Germans fought not against communism but against the Russian people. The Germans tried to humiliate us, to destroy us, and to make us slaves. As a German soldier said once, Hitler and Stalin were mad dogs. If one could place them both on opposite sides of a scale, it was unknown who would outweigh whom. It would balance perfectly. The thirst for power without regard to bloody excess was the principal motivation of these maddened beasts. Our people understood the situation.

The Germans drove the Jews into ghettos and forced them all to wear a Star of David. Many Jews who had fled from Poland after it was divided into Nazi and Soviet halves knew what the German occupation would bring for them and tried to flee into the depths of the country. There was no organized evacuation, for even the defending army itself was retreating in disarray. Denunciations of former Party members and of Jews in hiding outside the ghettos began. All of these people were arrested and shot.

Our people had to be "thankful" for the "wise leadership of the Party and of Comrade Stalin personally." Yet this sly tyrant later discovered how to revive the true national spirit, faith, and dignity: he ordered the reintroduction of the old tsarist military uniform. He conveniently forgot that a quarter of a century earlier, during the Russian Civil War, the epaulets of soldiers and officers who were taken prisoner by the Bolsheviks had been literally nailed to their shoulders. The old military decorations such as the Order of Suvorov were reintroduced as well.

Stalin also authorized the churches to be reopened. The majority of the churches had been blown up with dynamite by the "builders of the new world." There were few priests, because they either had perished in the harsh conditions of the concentration camps or had been shot for defending their faith. Those churches still standing had been desecrated by the Soviet authorities and converted into workshops, storehouses, or dance halls. Now the "wise leader" was opening them. They found "priests" who sang the popular song "Katiusha" at the altar in a half-drunken state.

Why was our Mother Russia being so cruelly punished? What other people could endure so much grief, hunger, fear, and infinite humiliation? Marching into battle, soldiers stopped shouting "For Comrade Stalin! For the Communist Party! For the Soviet Motherland!" Going into battle, the soldiers proclaimed new sayings: "For the sacred Motherland! For our Fatherland!" A wise change: how our poor Ivan[8] believed in it!

The Germans set up an occupational government in our district, commanded by two men sent from Poland. Two well-groomed men who spoke German and Polish, they both regarded the needs of the population cynically. No one received any help from them, but they themselves lived in high style. They arranged receptions and organized orgies.

Once, before my husband's arrival, I had gone to the district council to obtain a permit for a liter of milk for my mother-in-law, who was seventy-five years old, and myself. After I told them of our difficult situation, the head man answered with a malicious laugh, "Yes, I see," glancing at my stomach. "Your husband is at war, he's fighting against the Germans, and you want us to help you?" I looked him in the eye with contempt and left his office without speaking another word.

We knew that the Germans loaded freight trucks with stolen goods appropriated from Jews and others and sent them somewhere. The livestock from the collective farms were at the district council's disposal. A dairy was opened so the Germans could get their milk, butter, and cottage cheese, while the local inhabitants struggled to remain alive by any means.

The roundups of young people became more frequent. Young girls and boys were sent as slaves to labor in Germany. When the Nazis examined our young women, they could not believe that ninety percent of them were virgins. Our young people were not morally dissolute, despite all that they had endured.

By chance, I had met a young female doctor named Lidiia, before Anton came home. She was a genuine beauty, both physically and spiritually. She had finished her internship at a hospital just before the war, married a doctor, and was herself expecting a child. Her husband had been mobilized, and she did not know his fate. She lived in Minsk and came here to see her parents. Lidiia's mother was an extremely old woman, almost blind. Her father, a retired medical assistant, was in better health. Since visits were very rarely made because of the fear enveloping all of us, the family didn't know of my acquaintance with her.

Gentle, with a quiet, beautiful voice, Lidiia expressed neither despair nor complaint. All the same, she said to me one day upon meeting me, "I will die soon, Lena, for I have rapidly developing tuberculosis."

"Don't talk like that, Lidochka. How will the baby survive without you?"

"May God grant that it be born before my death," she said calmly. A daughter was born to her a few weeks later.

Although my husband's arrival should have cheered me, various complications began to affect my health and worsened until I was not able to rise from my bed. Anton carried me in his arms out to the garden for a breath of fresh air. A swelling formed under my armpit, by the breast, then spread to the breast itself. I became feverish and began to lose consciousness periodically. There were no doctors, and we certainly could not expect help from the authorities.

The swelling under my armpit and on part of my breast turned into an open wound, oozing pus. The family later told me that until the abscess burst I was delirious for about four days. Regaining consciousness, I suggested to my husband that he take me to Lidiia's father. The old medical assistant took his scalpel and began to scrape away the pus from inside the open wound immediately, without any conversation. Crying out from the pain, I lost consciousness. Liquid ammonia, held under my nose, revived me. We had to call on this kind-hearted old man several times to change the dressing.

In the meantime, Lidiia lay in bed, the days of her life cruelly numbered. Her face had become waxen like a dead person's, and she was not able to clear her throat.

"I have no strength, Lenochka! If everything is well with you and you recover, don't abandon my family, my daughter. Help her as much as you can." I gave her my word that I would help them as much as I could.

My mother-in-law treated me by her own simple method, with herbs of some kind. The efforts of the medical assistant, my mother-in-law, and most important the strength of my will to fight and to live gradually revived me. Slowly recovering, I began to come to the table.

"Thank God that I'm with you, Lenok. What would have happened if you had been alone now?" my husband said comfortingly.

One night I had a strange dream in which Lidiia whispered to me, "Farewell, I am leaving. Don't forget what you promised me, Lena." I looked at her lying in the middle of a room on a narrow bed, wearing a light blue crêpe-de-chine dress. She looked so beautiful. At that moment I awoke.

That morning I sent Anton to find out how Lidiia was feeling. Returning from the village, he didn't stop by the house but went directly to the barn and began work on something there. He couldn't fool me; I knew that Lidiia had died and he did not want to tell me. When he came into the house, I asked him, "When did she die?"

He faltered and then quietly said that she had died the previous evening. Her body lay at the house, and the neighbors helped her parents wash and dress the body. "They will bury her after lunch," he continued. "I will go to the funeral."

"Tell me, what was she dressed in?"

"In a light blue dress."

I had never seen her in this dress—how could I have dreamt that?

"Farewell, poor Lidiia! May your native earth lie light on you. Forgive me that I can't accompany you on your last earthly journey," I sobbed in a quiet voice. I remembered her beautiful face and the light blue dress for a long time.

God only knew what else might happen to all of us. I never worried for myself, for I had always managed to scramble out of the most difficult situations and serious illnesses. Now a horrible foreboding about Anton's life haunted me. Some internal voice kept telling me, "You will lose him, he will leave you!"

"But what could happen?" I asked myself. I knew that my husband loved me. He worried about my health and didn't sleep many nights so that he could ease my suffering. What else could happen? Why did my voice keep warning that he would leave me? Everywhere, every minute, every hour these horrible thoughts filled my heart.

Helen, 1947
Bavaria

Helen, John, Peter, 1947
Bavaria

Daughter Ena, 1947
Bavaria

Helen, 1967
Iowa City, Iowa

Ena, 1970
Canada

Professor Helen Dmitriew, 1992
Fresno, California

CHAPTER FOUR

SORROWFUL STRUGGLES

1

November 1941 came. It had not yet snowed, but the light frosts had begun, freezing the mud on the roads. Occasionally, a cargo truck would drive out of the district from Minsk, and a few residents were able to get into the city to obtain necessities at the flea market. Nevertheless, people had nothing. Even a bar of soap was considered a luxury.

We had nothing for the child we were expecting—no diapers or baby blankets or baby clothes. We had used all the bed sheets in treating the wounded soldiers. Anton decided to go to Minsk, hoping that he would be able to buy something there. The city dwellers were starving and in need of foodstuffs, so we knew that a piece of salt pork would be valuable currency to use for purchases.

Anton went to the district council and requested permission to go to Minsk via a passing truck. They promised him passage, but when he went the next morning there was no free space in the truck bed. He returned home disappointed, but I was glad. He was determined to go, however, and a few days later, telling no one of his plan, he rose early and set off for the council. This time he was able to get to Minsk. When I awoke and realized where he had gone, I still hoped deep down that they would not take him, that he would be back home in a few hours. By the time he had been gone the whole day, my heart began to beat uneasily.

The truck, with its load of people, was to return in the evening. The shadows became darkness, but Anton still didn't return. There was nothing we could do; nighttime curfews prohibited anyone from being on the streets, and the Germans would shoot without warning. I paced about the room, from one window to the other, the whole night.

Dawn came. Vanda entered the room. She had not slept the whole night either and tried to persuade me to lie down, fearing that I would become ill again.

"What should we do, Vanda?" I asked worriedly.

"We'll go to the council and find out whether the truck returned," she answered.

Instead of going herself, Vanda sent her cowardly husband. We were worried, because attacks by thieves were becoming more frequent. Bandits preyed on pedestrians along the forest roads and took everything. Armed men often stopped trucks and drove them into the forest, taking the passengers as well as the drivers.

Where was he? What happened? Why did he even go? Questions, questions, all without answers. My fears that I would never see him again, that I would lose him forever, began drifting into my mind.

My mother-in-law, almost blind in her old age, brought me some clothing that needed mending. I took up one of Anton's shirts, threaded a needle, and made only one stitch when I thought, "He'll never wear it again!"

"No! No! Don't think like that, you foolish pessimist!" I scolded myself.

Like an echo, however, the alarming refrain "he'll never wear it again, never wear it again!" still rang in my head.

Evening came, and I didn't turn my eyes away from the window. Suddenly, a mounted man came up to our house, opened the gate, and led his horse into the yard.

"Who could this be?" I asked myself. I had never seen this man before. "He's bringing me terrible news of my husband" went through my head like a clap of thunder.

I opened the door. The man gave his name.

"I am a friend of Anton's. We studied together at the university. I'm bringing you bad news. Anton is seriously wounded, but he is still conscious," he said, looking me directly in the eye.

"Where is he? Where is he?" I asked, choking from the tears and the lump in my throat.

He named the village, which was about ten kilometers from us.

"If you'll excuse me, I must hurry, because it's getting dark, and I want to go to my aunt's to spend the night there. I only hurried here to tell you what happened. I was riding along a road by the village when a *kolkhoznik* led by a cart with Anton in it, wounded.[1] He was crying out from the pain and was bleeding. When I rode up to the cart, I recognized Anton, and he recognized me and implored me to hurry and inform you. He's lying in the waiting room of a former doctor. The doctor is no longer there, but an apothecary gave him first aid."

Having said this, he rode away. When I entered the house, Anton's mother asked me questions: who was this and what did he want? Seeing the tears in my eyes, she became concerned.

"Mamochka, Anton is wounded. He's waiting for me."

She threw up her hands and began to cry. "What will we do now? It's already dark!"

We both went into Vanda's room to discuss what to do. Vanda and I decided to leave at daybreak and go to him. The night passed in terrible agony. "Perhaps he is already dead! Who wounded him? Why?" My internal voice literally screamed at me, "He is yours no longer. He will leave you forever."

"No, no, it can't be! He can't leave me!" I cried. "Oh, God, save him, don't leave me completely alone!" But the voice in my head wouldn't relent and kept repeating the same thing.

My body trembled all over from such nervousness and tension. I even ceased to hear my child's heartbeat. I became frightened, because it seemed that I was losing the two closest to me at once. I tried as much as I could to calm myself, but it was no good. It became hard for me to speak coherently. My mother-in-law sat next to me and asked that I pray and trust in fate. She then broke down in tears. Anton was her only son.

At three o'clock in the morning I suggested to Vanda that we set out on the road.

"But it's still very dark, and they will kill us," she implored.

"Let them kill us. I can't bear it any longer," I said fearlessly. "If you won't go, I'll go alone!" However, I knew that I couldn't go alone since I didn't know the way to the village.

We left the house an hour later and headed for the bushes that grew on the edge of the village. It was still dark, but it was safer to walk against the background of the bushes. It was snowing and a strong wind was blowing. Dogs' howls from a neighboring village seemed to be a harbinger of something horrible to come. Though the Germans were killing all the dogs, a few apparently still remained.

It was difficult to walk. My mother-in-law had forced me to dress very warmly, but along the road I began to take things off—first the warm kerchief from my head, then the sweater from beneath my jacket. Vanda walked in front, and I followed behind her, stumbling over the hummocks. We walked through the marsh, which was already frosted over. It was ten kilometers to the village by the road, but of course we couldn't go directly so our trip was much longer. It was soon light, but the village was nowhere in sight.

"Vanda," I asked, "do you know where we are going and where we are now?"

She was silent, knowing that we had lost our way. There was a bitter taste in my mouth, and my strength completely left me. I forced my legs to move only by sheer will. We walked on for a long time and finally saw a moving freight train going toward the front. After a few minutes, a passenger train to Minsk went by. Vanda brightened, for she knew that the railroad ran by the village where we were going.

We reached the village at about ten o'clock in the morning and asked a passerby where the doctor's waiting room was. As we headed for it, he turned back and shouted to us that the doctor was no longer there, since he was a Jew and they had taken him and his family away. He then repeated that the room was not far.

When we arrived, we found my husband in the waiting room without any supervision at all. Lying on his stomach and moaning loudly, he recognized us. About twenty-two hours had already passed since he had been shot, but he was still fully conscious.

"Lenochka, save me. All my hope is in you. I want to live. I want to stand on my feet again, to avenge myself against the enemies who are killing us like flies."

"Antok, don't speak of vengeance now. I will do all that is in my power to save you."

He was lying on a narrow bed, covered with a blanket. I lifted the blanket and saw a bloodstained dressing on his back. The bandages were saturated with coagulated blood. Blood from his abdomen had seeped through the thin mattress, and there was a large pool of blood on the floor.

He was nevertheless able to tell us that he had bought a few small things at the flea market, including some ribbons (for now he expected a girl to be born). He then went to the designated spot in Minsk, where the truck was to pick him up and waited until nightfall. The truck didn't show up, and Anton thought that something had happened. He then had to rush to his relatives' house before the curfew to spend the night with them.

Early the next morning, he left the city and decided to walk along a back road instead of the main highway. "It's not so terrible to walk forty kilometers," he had thought to himself. "After all, I've already walked five hundred kilometers, so this short distance is nothing. I'll be home by evening."

This was not unusual, for he was healthy with a strong, handsome build. Often, when we walked together and he took his long strides, I would have to run to keep up with him.

On the way home he dropped in on some friends who entertained him as best they could. After resting, he set off again with the happy thought that he would soon be home in the circle of his beloved family. While walking toward this village, he heard shots. He looked around and decided that the Germans were shooting on a firing range somewhere. Quickening his pace, he suddenly noticed that bullets were kicking up the dust of the frozen ground around him. He turned toward the origin of the fire and was about to throw himself to the ground when at that very moment a bullet hit him and he fell. The bullet passed through his abdomen next to his navel and went out through his spine.

Anton had been shot at from half a kilometer away by German railroad guards. Being drunk, they were arguing about whether they could hit a live target at such a distance. While Anton was lying in a pool of blood on the road, they ran up to him and said to him in broken Polish, "The hole is a small one. You'll live!"

The Germans stopped a peasant who was driving by, put my wounded husband in the cart, and ordered the man to take him to a doctor. The peasant later said that Anton had cried out frantically from the hard jolting along the frozen ground and that his blood had run out onto the road. During the trip, Anton's former university friend had ridden up on his horse, recognized Anton, and then come to tell me.

"What can I do now?" I asked myself. Anton asked for water, but I knew that with such a wound he should not drink. I instructed Vanda to moisten his lips and hold a wet cloth to his mouth, and then I headed for the substation, hoping to receive some kind of help from the Germans. The head of the railroad guard heard my story and promised that the first train going to Minsk would be stopped and that we would be able to take Anton to a hospital.

Returning to the waiting room, I told Anton and Vanda this news and hurried off to the village to find a cart to transport Anton to the substation. I made arrangements with an old peasant who was sympathetic to my grief. He himself had two sons somewhere in the war, and only God knew whether he would see them alive again. After laying straw on the floor of the cart to soften the jolts of the road, we drove off to the substation.

Whereas before I had no strength to move because of hunger and pregnancy, now I was running and felt almost no fatigue. My grief and nerves pushed me.

With great difficulty we loaded Anton into the cart and took him to the substation to wait for a passing train. Although Vanda and I earlier had seen many trains going in various directions, several hours passed. I sat next to Anton

and moistened his dry lips. Soon Anton began to rave periodically and lose consciousness.

Once, regaining consciousness, he told me that he
couldn't feel his body, beginning at the small of his back. He
was paralyzed. We turned him and placed him on his back.
I put my ear to his abdomen and heard not the slightest
sound. This meant that his stomach wasn't working; it was
clear that this would lead to peritonitis and further complications.

We spent the entire day waiting for trains that never
came. At last, when it was starting to get dark, a freight train
going toward our home appeared. The head of the guard
suggested it would be better for us to go to our own district
since it would be easier to arrange transportation from there
for Anton. Seeing no other way, I agreed. The train was
stopped, and we placed my husband on an open flatcar,
while Vanda and I sat at his head.

When the train arrived, Anton's sister and her husband (who lived and worked at the station) were there to
meet us. We carried Anton into their apartment on the second floor and placed him on a bed, which had been prepared
on the floor.

Anton's face was unbelievably red, meaning he had
developed a high temperature. Regardless of the darkness,
not fearing the German patrols, and prepared to sacrifice my
life and the life of my unborn child to save my beloved husband, I ran to the head of the district council.

The head of the district council was a new man, re-
placing the former head who had recently been arrested,
along with his assistant. This new man had been a political
prisoner, and I was acquainted with his wife, who was an
intelligent and very pleasant woman.

A police sentry stood guard by the council head's
home, and I had to explain the reason for my visit. Members
of the Soviet underground often killed men in his position.
The council head opened the door, and I told him everything.
He immediately dispatched the sentry to summon the driver
of the truck. The man arrived but flatly refused to drive at
night, saying the truck was in need of repair: the tires were
old and the motor was in wretched condition.

The driver then told me that two tires had gone flat in Minsk two days before, which caused him to miss picking up Anton at the appointed place. He now convinced me that we would break down on the road and would not be able to reach Minsk. Of course, the driver's fear for his own life played a big role. Indeed, it was dangerous to go out on the street beyond the corner of one's own home, let alone to travel on the road at night.

The head of the council then told me that a woman doctor lived not far from his home. I had not known about her. She had apparently gotten stuck in our village while retreating from the Germans. Accompanied by a policeman, I returned to the station with the doctor. As she examined my injured husband, I understood the hopelessness of the situation from her serious and preoccupied expression. I nevertheless tried to kindle some kind of hope for a miracle.

When we took off his blood-covered clothes, he took his belt, which was pierced by the bullet, and held it out to me. "Lenochka, take care of this belt. When our daughter grows up, you will tell her that her father died from this bullet." This struck me as strange, for he had always spoken of a son.

"My dear, my beloved, you will be alive, you will see your daughter yourself," I said to him, but an internal voice told me differently: "He is leaving you forever."

"No, Lenok, I must part from this life," Anton said weakly. "Take care of yourself, love my daughter, don't abandon my relatives, who love you. Arrange your life as best you can; you have to live in the name of our child, our daughter."

Anton again talked about a daughter instead of a son. How could he foresee the sex of our child?

"Forgive me if I have ever hurt you," he continued. "You were for me the brightest, most joyous ray in life. Your love and warmth smoothed all the roughnesses, all the unpleasant moments in it. You and I had so much in common. What a pity that the war cut everything short." He periodically closed his eyes while saying this.

"Oh, how I still want to live!" He became silent. It had become harder for him to speak.

At ten o'clock the truck drove up. We put the bed in the truck and carefully placed Anton on it. I don't remember how long it took us to drive to the hospital, but when we arrived there was almost no activity at all outdoors. I ran inside and saw that people lay everywhere in the corridors. Some cried out; others lay with open mouths and shut eyes, waiting for death.

Before the war this had been a large hospital with many well-known specialists. The majority of them had been Jews, and the Germans had already managed to send some of them to "the other kingdom." A few specialists were held in isolation. Therefore, the hospitals were almost totally without doctors.

The stench was intolerable. The tired nurses could scarcely move. I rushed up to one of them and, speaking rapidly, explained to her what had happened. She looked at me indifferently and only said, "Look, these are wounded brought from places where there are partisans. These are all accidental victims of the partisans' revenge or of reprisals by the German punitive squads."

"I want to see a doctor," I demanded.

Not saying a word to me, she started down a corridor. I followed closely, often having to step over the patients who were lying in the hallways. I had to speak to a doctor. The nurse went into a different part of the hospital and knocked on a door. She knew that I was following behind her, but we walked in silence.

The door opened to the office of Dr. Alekseev. Sensitive, compassionate, but at the same time helpless, Dr. Alekseev looked piteously exhausted. Having heard me out, he ordered that a place be found in the ward.

"There isn't a single free space," objected the nurse.

"Find one!" he shouted.

She left his office silently with me behind her. The nurse instructed the orderlies to bring Anton in on a stretcher. They placed him near her desk, where she wrote down all the information she needed. After a little while, they carried him to the ward.

"We have found a place!" I thought. "Perhaps a man

just died on his bed or perhaps they discharged someone," but at least Anton was in the ward.

Dr. Alekseev came. He removed the bandages from Anton's spine and from his abdomen. They asked me to leave, but I began to protest.

"You can't look at wounds in your condition," said the nurse.

"I've already seen hundreds of wounds and have given first aid myself," I objected.

The doctor silently examined Anton, who lay with his eyes closed. He wasn't speaking any more; he was unconscious. I noted the small wound in the middle of his abdomen and the quite large one right in his spine. The wounds were again covered with dressings.

"Doctor, I want to know everything. Tell me the truth," I demanded.

"There is little hope. Damaged intestines are a serious matter. We can expect a whole series of complications," the doctor gloomily explained to me. "When was he wounded?"

"The fourteenth of November at one in the afternoon," I answered.

"And today is the sixteenth, so two whole days have passed," the doctor emphasized and left the ward.

What the doctor didn't tell me was that the greatest danger to Anton was caused by the wound in the spine. I later noticed moisture on the bandages that was not blood and told the nurse. Cerebrospinal fluid had begun to drain internally. Lacking necessary medicines, they couldn't even consider operating.

Other than Vanda and myself, none of Anton's relatives was there. Later, two more of his sisters arrived. One of them had brought a fifteen-ruble gold piece that we sold on the black market so we could obtain medicine that the doctor had prescribed. Anton opened his eyes from time to time and seemed to recognize us.

On the third day, however, the convulsions began. It was impossible to restrain him, and he threw us off like wood chips. A doctor and an orderly came and began to make punctures in his spine with a large-bore needle, to reduce the pressure on the brain. Anton cried out from the pain. An inflammation of the cerebral membrane had begun, and then the brain itself started to swell.

On the fourth day he lay quietly, breathing unevenly.

On the fifth day his breathing was irregular, and I sat on a chair next to him all the time, applying a cold towel to his head. I wiped his cheeks with cold water. Suddenly he began to move and placed his head in my lap. His head was very heavy and pressed on my abdomen. I tried to put his head on the pillow several times. Finally I took the pillow off the bed and put it in my lap, so that he could rest his head on it.

He then began to make rasping sounds, and soon his breathing became less frequent and quieter. It quieted completely and a sharp beat of his heart followed, which made his entire chest shudder.

He was dead. It became clear to me that he had wanted to die in my arms.

Thus the kind heart of yet another victim of this war ceased to beat. This man who had never harmed anyone, who had loved his homeland, his people, and (although he had kept it a secret) his God, was dead.

I was completely numb, as if my life had stopped when his did. It felt as though a huge mountain had fallen on me and was pressing on me with its weight. I tried to believe that this was only a terrible dream and that I would awaken to find us together again. His sisters sobbed and looked at me with puzzlement. I was a frozen statue, unable even to cry.

Only fragments of their conversation reached me: " . . . what shall we do now . . . how will we get the body home . . . ?" I then became alert and ready to take the necessary steps. I explained in a trembling voice what I had decided to do. Only then, when the implications of "send the body" became clear, did the tears begin to flow.

"You promised me that you would never, ever leave me!" I wailed. "How could you leave me, to leave me alone again in torments?" My sobbing gradually began to die down.

Faces of people whom I had not long ago tried to help began to appear before my eyes, distorted by the pain of

predeath convulsions. It had been terribly painful then for
me to look at all of them. Now the pain was a thousand times
sharper. The man so close had been taken away from me.
Life seemed impossible without him.

I thought of the Russian maiden in I. S. Turgenev's
"Threshold," who answered these questions. Like her, I also
was ready for anything life dealt. Indeed, how much I had
already endured! How cruel fate had been to me from my
very childhood! Amidst all these torments had been one
bright ray, my husband. Now black clouds hung over me
again. Nothing remained but the endless struggle.

Yet the incredible strength that the Most High gives
us compelled my heart to beat and urged me to proceed.
What strength is concealed in human beings! How much can
one suffer and emerge the victor over torments, violence,
and immeasurable grief?

I knew from my conversation with the truck driver
where the district truck usually stopped. It was quite far from
the hospital. I explained to my sisters-in-law what needed to
be done, and Vanda and I headed for the place where we
would be able to catch the truck.

We had to walk for a long time. My feet didn't want
to move. My whole body was wooden. We saw that several
people from our village were already awaiting the truck as
well. These were people who engaged in sales (or, more accurately, resales since they speculated to survive).

The truck came before long, and people were already
sitting in its bed. The driver told us that he was overloaded
and could not take the dead body as well as the four of us,
but several female passengers interceded on my behalf. We
brought a long board out of a destroyed house, laid it the
length of the truck bed, and headed for the hospital. The
orderlies carried the body out, wrapped in a blanket, and laid
it under the board. My sisters-in-law and I sat on the board.

My dear Anton had departed for Minsk healthy and
full of hope and optimism for a better future. Just a week
later, we brought his body back to where he had been raised,
enveloped by the love of all his family.

To prepare Anton for his final journey, one of his
sisters brought out a new suit, shirt, and tie that had be-

longed to her husband, who was missing in prison. Observing all the traditions of the religious rites, the body was laid in the middle of a room in the part of the house where Vanda lived. On the twentieth of November Anton's body was committed to the earth, next to the grave of his father, who, ironically, had been killed by another enemy: the NKVD interrogator. Both deaths were glaring examples of violence and terror that reigns when human life is assigned no value whatsoever.

At the grave side, Anton's mother said tearfully, "You have taken my place, my little son!"

I only vaguely remember the day of the funeral. I was later told that they had to restrain me physically, for as they were lowering the coffin I tried to jump in the grave after it. They took me home only half alive.

I did not touch food for several days, no matter how my relatives tried to appeal to me in the name of my child. I kept Anton's belt with the bullet hole in my pocket and hardly spoke with anyone. My husband's relatives suspected that I was capable of taking my own life, and it seemed to them that I wanted to do so. They were wrong. Although I was confused and didn't want to live without my beloved husband, I certainly didn't want to kill myself.

I searched for some means to soften the soul-rending pain of my loss. I tried smoking and was quickly convinced that this was not for me. I tried alcohol, and it was immediately clear that this was not the way out. Only one alternative remained: to accept all of fate's blows without surrender and to carry my heavy cross.

I contemplated the purpose of life: "Why live? Where will I go and what will I do?" My internal voice replied, "Do what every sufferer does; struggle for your life, go by the road that fate shows you!"

"Where will I get so much strength to endure all of these difficulties?" I asked myself. But I knew of an inexhaustible strength that replenishes us in our weakness and spurs us to further struggles and suffering. It blesses us with a fleeting joy, which was to take form in the appearance of my unborn child.

2

Following the death of my husband, the wartime terror continued. The partisans—members of the Soviet resistance—regularly came out of the forests at night, captured men and young women, appropriated livestock, and stole what clothing and scarce food they could find. The partisans blew up railroads and derailed trains. By day German punitive squads roamed the countryside, burning down entire villages. For each of their comrades killed on duty, the Germans took revenge by shooting entire village populations and burning all the dwellings to the ground. Only the brick chimneys of burned houses remained in the German-occupied territories around the railroads.

The Soviet resistance tried to retaliate for the German atrocities as best they could, but the defenseless population suffered all the more. Rarely were assassins from either side caught. The slogan "the worse, the better" captured the spirit of the partisans. The worse the offense, the more the Soviet war effort would be aided through the hatred of the Germans.

Many of the so-called *pripisniki,*[2] who had managed to find temporary refuge during the retreat, were transported to work in Germany. Others still managed to escape to the forest and joined the growing numbers of partisan detachments. There were high-principled Communists among the partisans, and there were also many slaves to the situation, driven by the German terror over the village population.

In the first days of the war, many peasants had said that, although the German invasion might not be an ideal fate, at least it was something new and different from the tyranny of the Stalinist years. Thus, they often met the German troops with bread and salt, a traditional custom expressing hospitality. Soon, however, seeing what was happening around them, these peasants became convinced that they were dealing with an enemy that aimed its invading sword not against communism as a system, but against the Russian people themselves.

It was evident that neither communism nor fascism

valued human lives highly. Both systems were built not on a creed of compassion and love of others, but on the opposite principle: godless violence and the bloodshed of innocents. Yet I did not condemn those who ran into the forest, driven not by any ideological beliefs but by the instinct of survival.

In such a thicket of lawlessness and danger I remained, as did millions of our people. The position of the populace was so precarious that it is difficult to describe.

Since Anton was of Polish ancestry, he still had relatives in that country. People were trying to get to Poland from our occupied regions in search of food, because our population was starving. I decided to try my luck there and set off for Poland, where my daughter Ena-Anna was born on January 8, 1942. A Polish woman helped me give birth in a cold pantry. In another skirmish with death, I clung to life without a doctor, and the life of my little infant also hung by a thread. I warmed my dying baby daughter at my own ill breast. As every mother defends her offspring, risking her own life, so did I in semiconsciousness defend her. In "The Sparrow," Turgenev says, "Only by it, only by love is life held and moves."

The appearance of my daughter on God's earth was the clearest, most joyful gleam in my grief. She became for me my guiding star, which I determined to keep in my sight and follow. When she was born, there came a period in my life when I had to think how to preserve that gift, that memory which my dear husband had left me. Engrossed in these feelings, I forgot for a time about the surrounding situation. Hunger, death, fear, fires of destruction, indifference to suffering surrounded us all. So passed the first year of my solitude. I was in Lodz and other cities but did not find any of Anton's relatives. Ill and with a sick baby, I returned to Anton's immediate family a short time later.

I was gradually beginning to recover. It was difficult without a job, but there was not even a remote possibility of working. Peasants who had survived imprisonment came to me, asking that I write applications for the return of property that had been taken away prior to the war. I advised them on how I thought they should proceed. My sympathies were on their side, of course, since my family and so many of my relatives had also been robbed during the Stalinist years. Many of those who turned to me for help didn't even know my name, simply addressing me as "teacher." Many of these unfortunate souls had returned from prison with shattered health, and a few who had resettled in their own villages died from the bullets and fires of the punitive squads.

Defenseless women also were targets of violence, perpetrated both by Germans and by some of our own local policemen. The chief of the local police gendarmerie in our village,[3] who also served as interpreter, was a Russian man named Vinokuroff. He used and abused his power fully, savagely stealing from widows. If he learned in a denunciation that a widow was keeping gold coins, he beat the victim nearly to death until he received what he demanded. Vinokuroff was a handsome man in appearance, but physical quality meant little, since he had no spiritual qualities. He reminded me of Stavrogin from Dostoevskii's *The Devils*.[4]

Vinokuroff's young wife was herself quite beautiful but spoke in a squeaky voice. She flaunted a squirrel coat one time and a sealskin coat the next, accessorized with felt overshoes and a fur cap. Of course, she was dressed in clothing taken from Jews, the wives of former officers, or other destroyed women.

Other lonely women, whose husbands were in the army with an unknown fate, took German lovers. Once one of these women said to me, "You are so young and beautiful, why don't you find yourself a German who would help you? After all, you and your child are starving and suffering."

"For me to do that," I snapped angrily, "I would have to put on a dog's skin, which I can't! They killed my husband, and yet I should form a liaison with them? Never! Let a hungry death come before disgrace and humiliation!"

One day my sister-in-law and I stopped by the cooperative where Germans exchanged textiles for dried berries and mushrooms. These goods were beyond our reach, but it was interesting to have a look. Vanda and I were standing and talking about the materials when suddenly someone touched my shoulder. I turned about and saw, to my horror, that Vinokuroff was standing before me.

"Which material do you like here?" he asked, with the sensual smile.

"None!" I replied sharply, and we headed for the exit. He grabbed me by the arm and with the same smile asked me why I lived so far away. "Have pity on my boots (so their soles won't be worn out)," he said. "I would so like to visit you."

"In the first place, I wouldn't tend pigs with you, and don't you dare call me *ty*." I underscored my feeling by addressing him as *ty*. "In the second place, don't worry . . . where I'm concerned, your boots will stay whole, as I will have nothing to do with you," I said distinctly in a rapid voice. He was such a cruel, soulless man, I wanted to have nothing to do with him.

"Never mind, you and I will meet again," he growled maliciously through his teeth.

Leaving the cooperative, I trembled all over. Vanda tried to calm me, but fear overwhelmed me. I had heard so many horrible things about him and knew that he beat people during interrogations and recommended to the German police whom to shoot. Almost none of those arrested came out alive.

Just as intense battles raged everywhere on the front, nature unleashed fury at home. Frosts and snowdrifts continued endlessly until I could no longer endure sitting within four walls. The nights were long, with darkness all around. There was nothing to read and no paper to write on.

One day I told my mother-in-law that I wished to visit my sister-in-law Stanislava, who—because her husband was an employee of the railroad—lived in an apartment on the second floor of the station. Not heeding her protests, I went. Stanislava made tea. We cried for a while and talked to our hearts' content, and too soon it was time for me to return home to feed my daughter.

Walking home, and reliving my short life with Anton, I dwelled on those joyous days we had spent together. We used to sing (although both of us had poor voices), and Anton played the guitar. In our free hours he played records and taught me to dance the tango, the foxtrot, and the rumba. Thinking of him, I thought also of my daughter, who resembled him so much that at times it seemed as if I saw him when I looked at her.

I entered the yard of our home still engrossed with such thoughts. Seeing me come, my mother-in-law ran out onto the porch in tears, threw up her hands, and in a trembling voice said, "Lenochka, the police came for you; they wanted to arrest you!"

"For what? What have I done?"

I had barely spoken when three policemen entered the yard. One of them lived three houses up our street. The trio had awaited my return there. Having stated my surname and Christian name, one of them delightedly announced that I was under arrest and grabbed the sleeve of my sheepskin coat.

"Don't touch me, you guttersnipe," I said, pulling away to the side, "I'll go myself. I don't even intend to ask why you are arresting me."

At this time my daughter, whom I called Anechka, began to cry from behind the partition. I tried to run to her, but another policeman grabbed me by the arm. I freed myself with a jerk and went to her. Kissing my little girl perhaps for the last time, I was ready to go. I felt neither fear nor a foreboding of death and didn't even begin to cry, although my mother-in-law broke into sobs as if mourning the dead.

We walked more than two kilometers, a snowstorm blinding our eyes. No one uttered a single word during the entire journey. When they took me into the police station, an officer sitting at a desk took information about me, and the duty officer took me into the chief of the gendarmerie's large office.

I considered the situation carefully, knowing that none of those arrested came out alive but instead were taken to the *glinishche*,[5] stripped of their clothing, and shot. Never having considered myself a heroine, I nevertheless felt no fear and decided to defend myself as best I could.

A desk for the German chief was on one side of the room. In the far corner, Vinokuroff sat at a table, looking at me with the same insidious smile. I knew that this was Vinokuroff's revenge. The thick rubber hose with which he beat people during interrogations lay on the edge of the desk.

I had seen the German chief of the gendarmerie on the streets of the village several times earlier. He was a plump man, of medium height, with a stiff face that never smiled.

Besides the fact that he beat—more accurately exe-cuted—prisoners, the Russian chief of police also served as an interpreter. His translation services weren't necessary for me, and he would have the chance to beat me later anyway. I addressed myself to the chief of the gendarmerie in German, requesting that I be able to speak with him without witnesses. The chief asked me why, and I indicated that I had weighty reasons for this request. He turned to Vinokuroff and asked him to leave.

"We will still meet," Vinokuroff said maliciously to me without a smile.

The chief invited me to sit, and the interrogation began. The first questions concerned my identity and the location of my husband. A whole series of questions dealt with my alleged connections and activities with partisans. My answers began to pour out like a river. I told him of my life, of my childhood, of my flight from Siberia, of my studies and torments, of the loss of my husband. I defended my life like a tigress. When I told the chief that my brother and my husband had been mathematicians and that all my male and female cousins had been teachers, he looked me directly in the eye with great interest. It turned out that he had also been a mathematician in Germany.

Suddenly he began to speak to me in pure Russian. This was a great relief for me. I didn't have to search for foreign words to defend myself.

"I have to say that neither the Soviet partisans nor you Germans have inspired in me any feelings of sympathy or respect," I said, answering his query about my so-called partisan activities. "The Soviets destroyed my entire family, took away my home, and exiled me to a sure death in Siberia. You Germans killed my husband. So tell me how I could be a supporter of either side? If there were a third force here, I would undoubtedly join it."

"But why has someone informed on you that you work in the underground?" he asked.

I told him of my unpleasant meeting with Vinokuroff

and his threats. I also let the chief know of Vinokuroff's participation in rapes and robberies and how he abused authority as chief of police. By killing innocent, often anti-Communist Russians, the Germans were only helping the other side and hurting their own cause.

The German then got up and walked to a large bookcase. Opening the door and with a sweep of his hand indicating the stacks of folders on the shelves, he asked me, "These are all denunciations. Why are your people this way? Why do they denounce one another?"

"In the first place, that's how the Soviet authorities have educated them for the extent of the entire postrevolutionary period," I answered truthfully. "In the second place, resistance members conduct their own work. The more people you execute, the greater the service you do them."

From the tone of this conversation, it became clear to me that this man still had a glimmer of kindness deep in his heart, regardless of his position. True, he was a cruel executor of fascist violence. Toward the end of the interrogation, however, he even said a few words about his own family. His wife had been paralyzed for several years. With their three school-age children, they had lived under constant bombardment. His openness surprised me.

Believing my promise not to tell anyone that he knew Russian, he called the duty officer and ordered him to escort me to the exit. I was free! They weren't going to execute me!

Walking out, I encountered two of my sisters-in-law and my mother-in-law, who was holding my little daughter in her arms. They had come to bid me farewell as I was taken to the *glinishche*. Arrested people weren't kept in the prison long, for their fates were usually decided immediately after the interrogations.

To my relatives, my freedom was a miracle from the Lord! Indeed, after I had left and thought everything over, I knew that I could have been executed for my barbed answers. Even the chief of the gendarmerie himself had pointed out that I had a very sharp tongue, to which I replied that I spoke only the sacred truth.

The next day a rumor reached us that Vinokuroff had been arrested and sent to Minsk.

The destroyed countryside, the burned villages, and the sorry plight of the innocent people formed a depressing scene. The thought of leaving there had occurred to me long before my experience at the gendarmerie, but I was afraid to express it to Anton's family, particularly to his mother. Before his death Anton had asked me not to leave them.

To maintain my determination to live, I had to do something. I chose to find my husband's distant relatives in Minsk. When I announced my decision, I was surprised that my mother-in-law supported my idea.

At the end of February 1943, I left the gates of our house with my little daughter and set out through a blizzard into the unknown. I was taking a risk, but there was no other way out.

It was difficult to walk to the station through the deep snow, but I eventually arrived at the station. My sister-in-law's husband helped me get permission to go by train. I entered the car, opened the door to the compartment, and gasped in horror. Vinokuroff and his wife were sitting in the compartment. They had released him from prison after ten days and transferred him to a job in Minsk. Such Russians were needed by the Germans; after all, not everyone was capable of torturing and killing innocent people.

My whole body trembled with fright, which made my little daughter begin to cry. I tried not to look to the side where Vinokuroff was sitting. His wife knew nothing of what had happened, but he knew why he had been arrested and who caused his temporary downfall. Now he could shoot me and answer to no one. One more victim would mean absolutely nothing. We traveled to Minsk in silence, stepped out onto the platform, and went in different directions.

Crossing the railroad at an intersection far from the station, I noticed the contorted, frozen corpses of prisoners. Not yet covered with snow, these corpses apparently had been discarded recently. My heart sank at the sight. Somewhere their mothers or their wives and children waited for them, yet they lay here stiffly with no one to bury them.

This setting kindled images in my mind of all the death I had seen inflicted on our people, from my personal experiences in the concentration camps of Siberia to the retreating Red Army soldiers killed in the first German air raids. The question raced through my mind again: why was our country being punished so, as if for a sin before God?

The old people said that we were being punished for our departure from God. I wanted to believe that there glimmered a wisp of faith and goodness in the very soul of the majority of our people (excepting, of course, those who quit their faith to serve the godless authorities devotedly).

With these weighty thoughts, I was able to find the house of Anton's father's cousin. Her husband had been arrested during the Stalinist purges and died in prison. They had informed her of his death but not of the circumstances. She lived with her daughter and rented a room to a woman with an eight-year-old boy.

The tenant, a Ukrainian who had been married to a Jewish doctor, had worked as a pediatrician before the war. Fearing for her son's life, she went into hiding, for the Germans killed even half-Jewish children. Living in my relatives' home, she helped orphans and homeless children, later opening a shelter in the same location as the kindergarten where she had worked before the war. She somehow was able to receive a scanty grant from the city to provide minimal support to these children, doomed otherwise to a hungry death.

Vera, Anton's cousin's daughter, worked in the kitchen at the terminal and managed to bring home soup and bread. Her life was complicated by the fact that, since she was a pretty blonde, the Germans who worked in the kitchen had their eyes on her.

Vera often cried. Before the war she had loved a university classmate, Serëzha, but he was now missing. She had no new information about him, but still she dreamed and hoped to see him alive.

When I arrived with my little daughter and told them all that had happened (they still didn't know of Anton's death), the lady of the house immediately invited me to stay with them, but there was no room. A few days later I met a Polish woman who lived across the street from my relatives. We began to talk, and I learned that her husband had been arrested and executed many years before and all their property, including the building with several apartments, had been confiscated.

During the war she was able to convince the city civilian administration (created by the German Command) to return the dilapidated building to her. She lived in one of its apartments with her sixteen-year-old daughter. The young girl was very pretty, which couldn't be said of her mother. Like thousands of others, she and her small child had suffered greatly, labeled enemies of the people. Not even having a piece of bread, they had starved and found shelter with others.

The decrepit and rundown building resembled the landlady herself, but with no other place to go, people lived in it. Her apartment had two bedrooms, a dining room, and a kitchen. I rented a room and communal use of the kitchen. As a condition of the rental payment, I agreed to help her obtain heating materials, but at the time I had no conception of the difficulty of this task: firewood was impossible to find in war-torn Minsk. I was ready to take on any demand to find some kind of shelter for myself and my little daughter. I also needed to find work, even if for only half a day.

The rations we received each week consisted of 1.4 kilograms of bread, which was sixty percent sawdust, and 200 grams of pearl-barley per person. It wasn't necessary to slice the bread since it fell apart on its own. Such was life in the city. At the flea market I exchanged a small loaf of bread for two dresses for my little daughter. She was already talking and, looking happily at the new things, said "pitty." She couldn't say the letter *r* for a long time.

Vera found a half-day job for me as a cleaning woman in the kitchen where she worked. They didn't pay us money, but it was possible to take home a small loaf of bread and the soup that remained after the meal. I contrived to bring my landlady a little coal and a few pieces of kindling in my cleaning pail. She and I shared the bread and soup.

Anton's sister Viktoriia and her family had since fled the city for the country. They took along only what could fit in a small cart and went on foot to my mother-in-law's home. Their other belongings, including blankets, dishes, and clothing, were left at my cousin's house. These things now proved

very useful, for my daughter and I had nothing except what
was on our backs.

Days turned into weeks, and weeks turned into
months. There was no official information on the war's
progress, so we could only surmise from the Germans' faces
that everything was not going smoothly for them. Soviet airplanes began to fly over the city more frequently, and the
Soviet resistance stepped up its activities, murdering more
and more German officers and soldiers, which resulted in the
Germans retaliating with acts of unbelievable terror.

One night a German officer was killed in the Koma-
rovka district, on the outskirts of the city. The next morning
a German detachment surrounded the area and led all its
inhabitants to the edge of the adjacent small woods. They
forced all the men and women on their knees so that they
were the same height as the children and opened fire with
machine guns, killing everyone without mercy.

One young woman escaped such a roundup by hiding
undetected in a cellar. She later told me that, when the Germans came, a woman who also lived in that house tearfully
asked to be allowed to bury her dead child, whose body lay
in a small coffin. "Bury him along with yourself" was the
abrupt response. The mother was taken away with the others
and killed.

Many single women were willing to do anything to
save their children and themselves from a hungry or tortuous
death. They washed the Germans' linen in exchange for a
piece of bread. The wife of a Soviet army colonel who had
disappeared stood for entire days on a central street and sold
Russian and Byelorussian newspapers. Some women, risking their lives, took up speculation, and others simply lived
with Germans, having sold their bodies for food and shelter.

Throughout the entire occupied zone, Germans
would force able-bodied young people to work in labor
camps in Germany. They lived in horrible conditions and
were forced to work beyond their strength. They suffered
beatings and endured every other conceivable humiliation.
The slightest offense would earn passage to the *kontslageria*.[6]

The occupying Germans humiliated all the native
population with their callous attitudes and vicious actions.

Even though they had met the Germans with bread and salt at the beginning of the war, Russian peasants now anxiously awaited the arrival of the Soviet troops.

"Out of the fire and into the flames," says the Russian proverb. Fearing death, I had fled the rural region, but again I was in the same dangerous situation. Life was not easy and death followed closely on the heels of everyone.

CHAPTER FIVE

TORN FROM THE MOTHERLAND

1

The spring of 1943 arrived. Snow still lay in muddy patches, but the ground peered through in places. It was cold, and when the wind blew you could feel the cold air whistling through the chinks of the old house.

Very early one morning, my landlady set off for the flea market. She speculated in the winter and sold vegetables from her kitchen garden in the summer. Her daughter helped her. I walked into the communal kitchen to make some kasha on the *trinozhka* for my daughter and noticed a small moving figure through the window.[1] A young girl in torn, ill-fitting clothing and large felt boots was heading toward our porch, trying to lift her feet high.

"A little man as big as your thumb,"[2] I thought, thinking of a poem by Nekrasov while opening the door and leading her into the kitchen without question. I realized why she walked through the kitchen gardens and not along the streets: she was hiding from those who pursued such children. This little girl was undoubtedly from a Jewish family.

She looked at me, her dark eyes pleading for sympathy and assistance.

"Where are you from, little one?" I asked, trying to speak as tenderly as I could. "Where do you live and where are your parents?"

At first she didn't answer and then slowly replied, "I have no mama and no papa."

"Then with whom do you live?"

After a pause, she told me that she lived in the cellar

of a destroyed house with several other children who were in hiding. There had been twelve of them at first, but hunger and cold took their toll so now there were only six. Their leader was all of thirteen years, and this little girl was only eight.

Standing close beside her in the kitchen, I caught the appalling odor of her mouth. I removed her ragged little coat. All of her clothing reeked of urine and was impregnated with dirt and lice. It was almost repulsive to touch her.

Immediately I threw her clothing into the stove to burn it and began to heat some water to wash her. I fed her what I could and dressed her in clean clothing that had belonged to Viktoriia's daughter. Her little face brightened. She wore large men's socks on her small feet, and I had to dress her in the same felt boots in which she had come.

"My God!" I exclaimed to myself. "It's me! It's me! This little girl is me in Siberia!" My heart filled with still more pity and compassion for this small sufferer.

When I bathed her in the small bath, I could see how her thin little body burned, eaten by the lice. I had felt these painful sensations myself, and I understood her pain. The only difference was that this little girl's misfortunes resulted from the work of a foreign enemy who had crossed our borders, while mine were the work of our own government's murderers.

"What is your name?" I asked.

"Esfir'."

I didn't ask her whether she knew how her parents had perished, since that was obvious.

When she left, she took with her a small tin of potato soup and a piece of bread, which was all that I could spare. "May you reach your 'own' place safely, little one," I thought, hoping they wouldn't catch her.

Closing the door behind her, I heard my own little daughter's voice. She had awakened and was calling for me. I entered the room, picked her up from the bed, wrapped her in a blanket, and pressed her firmly to my breast.

"Lord, never let my daughter be left an orphan," I prayed. "Give me the strength to endure all adversities and put me on the path of truth; help me to be strong so that I will be able to help those in need. Help the little orphan children, warm them with your affection. Don't let the enemies take their lives away."

So in the depths of my soul did I call out to God. I wanted to sob, but the warmth of my daughter filled my heart, and her guttural but happy chirping brought me out of my painful reflections.

Several days had passed when two small girls appeared from behind the barn and came up to the porch. Esfir' had brought Roza, a six-year-old friend in misfortune. Roza spoke little but followed my every move. Both were hungry and trembling from the cold. I fed and warmed them, and they left. Their visits became more frequent. I learned from the girls' conversation that the oldest boy in the group—their leader—had died. In spite of my landlady's objections, these two girls continued their visits.

"Do you know what you're doing?" she shouted at me. "You're exposing us all to danger!"

I knew very well that each time these little girls came to the building, my life and the life of my daughter hung in the balance. "But what do you want me to do with these little ones?" I protested. "They are innocent children! Imagine your daughter in their place!"

She apparently mentioned my activities to the three tenants who lived in the basement. These two sisters and their alcoholic brother were rumored to have been nobles in the past. The landlady was very well inclined toward them, since her own husband had been from the nobility.

Walking by the basement tenants' door one day, I heard a man's voice coming up the stairs.

"I know you're helping Yid kids," the alcoholic brother snarled. "Do you understand what that means? If you don't bring me a bottle of vodka, I'll inform on you to the Germans. The choice is yours; either the bottle or . . ."—he didn't finish.

I shook with anger. "I'm helping defenseless children! I don't know what their nationality is . . . these are children! Do you understand? Children!"

"It's your business," he said. "I have given you my conditions."

I somehow had to obtain vodka, and the only place to get it was at the flea market. I always went there with great apprehension, even when I only had to buy a half liter of milk for my daughter. Sometimes the Germans organized roundups, seizing young people and sending them to Germany. At other times the local police surrounded the flea markets and took away for themselves all the goods and food that people had brought to sell or trade.

I wondered what I could exchange for the vodka. I had nothing of value except the warm blanket that had been Viktoriia's. Putting it in a bag, I set off, trembling with fear.

When I got to the flea market, I traded the blanket for a piece of salt pork. The salt pork I traded for vodka. The man who pulled a half liter bottle from under the table looked at me doubtfully. He must have thought I was quite an alcoholic, if I traded a precious piece of salt pork for vodka. Returning home, I descended the stairs to the basement lodgings and gave the bottle to the alcoholic extortionist.

The poor orphan girls continued to visit periodically. I helped them as much as possible, even sharing my last piece of bread. This was their only opportunity to get hot food and warm themselves, albeit temporarily.

Months dragged by without a single glimmer of hope in our lives. Everything was the same: cold, hunger, and the threat of death hanging over our heads. Thanks to Vera, I was still able to work a little in the kitchen at the terminal. When leaving for work, I would shut my daughter in our room. Returning home, I would often find her sleeping on the cold floor. She was frequently sick and coughed all the time.

Our land was soaked with the blood and tears of these victims, who were guilty of nothing. Millions had died during the Stalinist purges of the 1930s, and millions more were murdered by the new enemy of the next decade. It is impossible to comprehend the torments that our people experienced during those years.

It remains a sad fact that the West paid no heed to the suffering of our people but, on the contrary, naively supported the Stalinist government. Though the roots of communism were not deep, they were poisonous and creeping, engulfing more and more victims like the tentacles of an octopus. Communism was a cancer on the body of humanity. Its leaders attributed all their deficiencies to others and feigned blindness to their own shortcomings. They exploited the people with calls for free labor to the state, all "for the good of the Party." Various government projects were built by the hands of slaves—its own citizens.

Reflecting on the fate of my people was unbearably painful to my soul. On the other hand, I knew their inexhaustible strength, mighty enough to endure this oppression and humiliation. Russians possess goodness, love, and hospitality. I believed that a future hour would arrive when the rage against the oppressors would pour forth, when the martyred would find freedom. Yet only those who struggle for life and freedom are worthy of them. Indeed, there is nothing in life dearer than freedom and life itself.

2

By a cruel twist of fate, late in 1943, I was rounded up by the Germans and cast into a horrible transit camp at Poznan in Poland. About 11 million people were forcibly removed from the occupied regions and sent to work. The Poles viewed the Russians with hostility because of Stalin's division of Poland with Hitler. On the other hand, because they also knew firsthand the terror of enemy occupation, the Poles eagerly awaited the arrival of the Soviet army to free them from Hitler.

It was impossible to sleep on the beds in the barracks. The straw mattresses, filthy blankets, and bunkbeds crawled with millions of bedbugs. The only difference from my earlier experience in Siberia was that it was not so cold here. I had my two-year-old daughter, and she had her helpless mother—we had only each other. Worst of all, we were no longer among our own people, but among foreigners.

After a while the Nazis sent us from Poznan to Königsberg in western Prussia, and then to Berlin, where we sorted vegetables in dark cellars, amidst terrible bombing.

Allied victory over the Germans became increasingly certain. Even many Germans expressed this prediction aloud.

I eventually ended up working on a farm four kilometers from Kempten, in Bavaria. The owner's large family and many relatives—German families who had fled Czechoslovakia and other places—ran this farm. Fourteen French prisoners of war also lived there, and a young Ukrainian girl named Annushka stayed in the basement with a family of Byelorussians. There were five people in that family: two old people, their grown son, their widowed daughter, and her eight-year-old son.

I liked Annushka very much and tried to protect her from the men's sly glances. She was only seventeen, with rosy cheeks, beautiful dark expressive eyes, and a pleasant smile, but she was naive. Because she was inquisitive and interested in everything, I tried to teach her to be ready for harsh reality, while holding herself to high moral standards.

Annushka had no fear of the landlord. She often drank some of the cream produced by the 130 dairy cows on the farm and even schemed to steal bits of the landlord's food. When he yelled at her, she responded in Ukrainian, asking him to kiss her in a particular place. Only once did he become so infuriated that he was ready to strike her. I blocked his way, standing between them. He then threatened me, but the matter ended there. All of us workers used to call him the Bull. We told this to the Frenchmen, who would warn us as we were working in the hothouses: "*Faites attention!*[3]—the Bull!"

It was a terrible environment. The German children, as well as the adults, were filled with hatred toward Slavs in general and Russians in particular. While playing outside, these children would deliberately push my daughter down and throw dirt at her. My heart ached whenever I saw this, but I had to wait until the end of the workday to comfort, wash, and feed her.

Under these conditions, my daughter fell ill once again, and it quickly became serious. I spent many sleepless nights with her, but continued to work in the daytime. I looked like a living skeleton.

Laboring for fifteen or sixteen hours a day, often

doing work beyond my strength, I still knew that the pain and exhaustion that I endured were not as terrible as the suffering of those dying on the war front or in the east from hunger and cold. Only those who have borne these things on their own shoulders can understand the kinds of horror war brings. There was nothing left for us to do but to be patient and hope for Allied victory.

On the evening of May 9, 1945, I had finished the daily laundry and was preparing dinner for the French prisoners when two American paratroopers appeared on the farm. Through the window, I saw how the English-speaking landlady, the daughter of a former general, smiled seductively at the approaching guests. The Frenchmen surrounded them and vied with each other to talk the Americans' heads off. After about forty minutes, the Americans walked off toward the woods.

After cleaning up the kitchen, I wearily climbed the stairs to my room at about eleven o'clock, to rest until my sick daughter awoke. The French prisoners were usually confined at night, but for some reason this night they were not. Suddenly, I heard hurried steps beyond the door. Two of the Frenchmen asked me to open the door so that they could eavesdrop on the voices outside. My room in the garret had a northern exposure. The voices were coming from the south, but there were still dreaded German SS troops hiding in the mountains, so the Frenchmen thought my window was the safest place to listen to the approaching voices.

We soon realized that we were hearing a language other than German. Before long we spotted four Americans, including the two who had been there earlier. The Frenchmen ran outside and embraced them as brothers.

Upon the demands of the Frenchmen, the landlord opened the wine cellar, which was filled with various bottles, even some rare hundred-year-old vintages, according to the Frenchmen. Soon shouts and singing drifted up from the first floor, followed by the smashing of glasses and dishes in the kitchen and landlord's dining room.

In my room over the landlord's bedroom, I could hear the landlord's sobbing. He had been cruel to the Frenchmen and to all us Slavs, but to me he sounded like a coward, now that he was in danger. When I heard his plea that he not be killed, a chill ran over my body and I whispered: "Oh, Lord, don't let them murder him."

Then I heard the cries and tears of the young German girls who were fulfilling their *Arbeitsdienst* on the farm.[4] The drunken Frenchmen were raping them. I pitied these young girls, in particular one who was especially gentle and sympathetic. The girl was from a cultured family, and I learned that she had even read many of our Russian classics in translation. When she was working with me in the kitchen, she often saw that I gave the Frenchmen whole milk instead of skim.

I was sorry that I couldn't come to the defense of these girls, but it would have meant one woman reasoning with eighteen intoxicated men—tantamount to talking with a bottle.

While pandemonium raged downstairs, I remained in my room and cradled my sick daughter in my arms. Her little head, ears, and parts of her face were covered with scrofula, which was threatening her eyesight. She was in great pain, and I suffered with her in my heart. Like every mother, I would rather have been sick myself, but I could give her no aid except to hold her in my arms and communicate love. By two o'clock in the morning she had fallen asleep, and I put her down on the bed and lay down next to her, although it was impossible to sleep.

Hearing the voices of the drunken Frenchmen approaching my door, I became instantly alert. They knocked on the door and told me that their "American comrades" wanted to see a "Russian madame." They always called me "Madame" or "Hélène." My whole body shook as I went to the door and opened it.

Two Americans and two Frenchmen, one bearing a couple of bottles of wine for me, came into the room. I was struck by the military uniforms of the two handsome paratroopers. They had pockets everywhere. One of the Americans, speaking in English, went to the bed and made a wreath of chocolate bars around my sick little girl's head. He said something else in English to me, but because I could not understand a word I simply answered in French, *Merci beaucoup*. The four of them then left the room.

Toward dawn, the uproar began to lessen. I opened the door and went out to the garret. The laundry I had hung the day before was strewn about, and the drunken men had walked all over it. Going toward the staircase, I tossed aside various garments, which had been thrown out of the wardrobes. When I entered the kitchen, I knew there would be no making breakfast, so I returned to my room and decided to await what would come.

At six o'clock in the morning, a Frenchman knocked on the door and said that we all had to leave the house.

At long last, the day of our freedom had come. Where could we go to find shelter? We didn't have money, clothing, or even a piece of bread! One of the Frenchmen offered to bring me the landlord's clothing, but I would not take his things. "We have survived up to now and will survive after now as well," I thought to myself.

The struggle continued. Confused and scared people ran into the forests or hid in the mountains. Although they were uncertain about the future, one goal was clear: not to fall back into the monster Stalin's clutches alive. Completely alone and helpless, I nevertheless sensed some invisible force pulling me along and saving me once again from death. As I conversed mentally with God, I felt His power and hope. Faith alone propels a weak and feeble person along the path of the fight for life.

Annushka had girlfriends in a camp for *ostovtsy* in the city and decided to go to them.[5] The Byelorussian family loaded their things onto a cart, and I set off with them toward the city as well. We plodded along the highway, looking around, not knowing where to stop. Along the southern side of the highway, we saw small houses constructed of cement blocks. I suggested that we investigate who lived in them and whether perhaps one was vacant. We later learned that these houses had been built for the survivors of the Allied bombings.

An elderly man was standing near one of the houses. Being a German from Poland, he spoke both languages. In talking with him, we found out that he managed the properties and could assign us to an unfinished house. There were seven of us in that small house (the five-member family plus

my daughter and myself), but we were very happy. We had
a roof over our heads and a stove.

Kontslagerniki and *ostovtsy* came out to freedom from
behind the barbed wire and pillaged storehouses and private
homes alike.[6] They stole clothing, fabric, and what food they
could find, often murdering those who stood in their way.

In the absence of rationing, we didn't know how we
could obtain necessities. We would not even think of resort-
ing to robbery. I decided to earn my slice of bread by sewing,
even though I had never even mended so much as a sleeve.
"If you want to live, find the means to adapt to the circumstances," I resolved.

The Byelorussians' grown son had been a mechanic
in the past. He found a burned sewing machine among some
scorched ruins. He dismantled it, repaired the parts, reas-
sembled the small arm, and made it usable. Annushka began
to refer customers to me, who needed dresses and skirts
shortened. I could tell that this clothing had been taken from
someone else's shoulders, for sometimes it was necessary to
rip an article completely apart and piece it back together. In
payment for my work, people brought bread, sugar, coffee,
or cheese. At least we did not starve. The old Byelorussian
woman prepared the meals, and her daughter helped with
the children.

Rumors that the Americans would return us to the
Soviet Union by force began to circulate. We didn't want to
believe that America would take such a step, but the Soviet
Repatriation Mission undertook its task with zeal. Some of
the mission's officers didn't hide the fact that these returning
ostovtsy would never again see their own homes. Nevertheless, with suitcases already packed, many *ostovtsy* eagerly
anticipated their return to the homeland.

Although many of our people detested communism,
this still did not mean that they supported fascism. These
former commanders and soldiers sought refuge from the free
countries, but were refused. The Allies closed their ears and
would not accept into their ranks these seekers of freedom.
As a result, innocent victims were sent, as into the jaws of a
boa constrictor, to a certain and dark fate.

The Treaty of Yalta, signed by Allied leaders in February 1945, bound the United States and Great Britain to extradite by force all former Soviet citizens back to their homeland. Stalin had been able to convince them that the expatriates were enemies of the people or Nazi collaborators, ignoring the fact that he himself had been the greatest collaborator. President Roosevelt and Prime Minister Churchill signed the death sentences of thousands of innocent Soviet citizens in order to please Stalin. The fate of the doomed was naively decided, even though they were guilty only of seeking freedom and the right to worship God. The West did not listen, did not want to listen, to the cries of the condemned.

During the extraditions, provocateurs would appear, either agents sent ahead by the KGB or refugees themselves hoping for Stalin's forgiveness in exchange for their treacherous services. Soviet KGB agents had access to the nonreturnee camps. On occasion, the more decent of them would warn those of us destined to be deported: "Run away! Death, prison, and Siberia await you."

Some of the nonreturnees, who either had served willingly in German units or were former political prisoners, were regarded by Soviet authorities as the most evil enemy of all. One cannot dispute the fact that a few Soviets served the Germans faithfully. Frequently, however, these collaborators had been secret informers in the militia before the war or former political prisoners from the Soviet *kontslageria*. As a policeman once said in justifying his savage and inhuman actions, "the blood of a policeman flows in my veins."

Like so many others, I had done nothing wrong, but I held the executioners culpable. My entire family had been destroyed, and the man I loved—my cherished husband and the father of my child—had been taken away from me. Was I guilty because of the fact that during the first strikes by the German enemy I had saved the lives of dying Red Army soldiers who had been abandoned in the fields to bleed to death? Was it that I had taken from my own mouth the last piece of bread, helping those who were dying of hunger? Or was it that, endangering my own life, I strove to save and protect the lives of those children doomed to death? Almighty God Himself bears witness to my acts and will be the final judge.

Yet God is not without mercy. At the United Nations, Eleanor Roosevelt came forward in answer to Soviet accusations that "criminals" (mostly women, children, and old people) were hiding in the western zones of Germany and Austria, spreading slander and propaganda against the Soviet Union. Mrs. Roosevelt defended the nonreturnees. Although the extraditions ceased, the distrustful refugees still strove to cover their tracks by changing their nationality, denying their prewar residence, and renouncing their native tongues.

In the confusion, complete chaos reigned in the refugee camps, and drunkenness and debauchery flourished. Having suffered so many beatings and other humiliations, the inhabitants of the camps "threw off their bridles" and unrestrainedly allowed themselves everything.

Annushka would come visit me with increasing despair reflected on her face. She was embarrassed by the unconcealed sexual passion of her contemporaries and was tormented by anguish for her family, whose fate remained unknown. Annushka remembered happier days and the broad Ukrainian fields where she had run with the other children, so she was considering the Soviet Repatriation Mission's offer to return home. The poor young woman didn't suspect that it was highly unlikely that she would end up in her home village and that the best she could hope for was the desolate and barren life in Siberia.

Hesitating in her decision, she came to me for advice. Unfortunately, I could offer her no comfort. As much as I wanted to keep her with me, I didn't have the right, since the future was not guaranteed. On the other hand, I couldn't tell her to go, since I knew where that road would lead.

"Annushka, do what your feelings tell you to do," I advised her. "If you stay with me, I will not leave you, and we will share what comes. But I can't make your decision, because you might blame me later for the outcome."

Five weeks passed. One day I decided to visit the camp. As I approached, I could hear wild, terrible shouts. They had found a former guard who had been in hiding since before the American units' arrival. This man had previously been in an SS unit until he was wounded and subsequently assigned as a guard. The inhabitants hated him for his excessive cruelty. When he was found earlier that day, a lynch mob passed judgment on him and simply tore him to pieces. I didn't dare go near the crazed horde.

Another group was forming behind a barracks. I went over to it and saw a young woman sitting on a bench, her head lowered. Some of the crowd reached out to pull her hair or shove her in the back.

"What's this about?" I asked bystanders.

"She's sold her hide! She's married a Frenchman and wants to go with him to France," a red-haired fellow with a pockmarked face irritably explained. I knew instinctively that the young woman's life was in danger.

"You're picking and yelling at her for that?" I asked incredulously. "The homeland needs people loving and faithful to the authorities, and she has fallen in love with a foreigner. Well, let her go with him. Maybe later she'll miss her homeland and will drag her Frenchman back there, too."

The crowd grew quiet.

"Why do you show foreigners that some of you don't want to return home? This doesn't look well at all," I continued.

Reverse psychology acted like a sedative on the drunken patriots, and they began to disperse. I walked up to the young woman. She was sobbing quietly and wiping the tears away with her hands. Her fiancé was sitting beside her with a frightened expression.

"Don't be a fool," I told her quietly. "Clear out of this camp before it's too late."

They looked at me solemnly, got up, and headed directly for the exit of the camp.

I then went to find Annushka. Entering the remote barracks in which she lived, I saw bodies moving beneath blankets on the bunkbeds lining the walls around the open room. "Neither shame nor conscience," I thought to myself and turned to leave. Near the exit, I saw Annushka. My "plump one," whom I had so carefully guarded, was lying in an upper bunk with some fellow with unfocused eyes and a drunken smirk.

"Annushka!" I cried out. "I can't believe it!"

"Why? 'A mouse gnaws what it likes!' " she answered blearily. Apparently she had made her decision.

I never went to the camp again. It was too painful to see those conditions and witness the downfall of our young people, forced by such circumstances. The war had caused all this. How many innocent victims and squandered souls!

Just before her departure, Annushka came and dropped to her knees before me.

"Forgive me!" she begged. "I've done such things that I don't even know how to look you in the eye!" She tearfully told of the terrible peer pressure and how that had been the first time she had tried alcohol.

My poor Annushka! I helped her to her feet, embraced her, and held her close. She again expressed doubts about her decision to return to her homeland, but my reply was the same as before.

"It is up to you. If you stay, you will be my daughter." My heart ached. I wanted to tell her to stay, but I couldn't take responsibility for that decision. We parted as sadly as would a mother and daughter. Both of us sobbed, knowing we would never meet again.

The next day, Annushka and others left for the dark unknown. The steam whistles of the train sang their song of farewell. I don't know what became of Annushka. I would like to believe that she and the thousands like her endured all the hardships of the Siberian camps and that their lives were spared by some miracle.

3

Following the Allied liberation, the process of registration began in the camps of nonreturnees. Because we knew almost nothing about emigration, we had never even considered the possibility of staying in the West, until we happened to meet people from the first emigration (or, as we used to call them, old émigrés).[7] Not all these old émigrés, however, enthusiastically offered aid to their Russian brothers and sisters.

Mostly Germans lived in the small settlement where my daughter and I stayed, but soon Poles, Byelorussians, and Russians settled in. The children spoke various languages, but predominantly German. They grasped other languages very quickly and often served as interpreters for their parents.

Once, while walking past a school that housed refugees from France, Yugoslavia, and Bulgaria, I saw several people standing on the street, conversing quite loudly in Russian. Hearing my native language, I rushed over to them, disregarding the rules of etiquette.

"Are you Russian?" I asked them joyfully. A tall woman examined me from head to toe with a frown. Evidently unimpressed by my miserable appearance, she asked me irritably, "And you are a Soviet?"

"No," I answered quietly. "I'm only a Russian."

A man standing next to her in a military uniform was clearly embarrassed by the woman's rudeness and politely asked me where I came from. I could barely hold back tears as I talked with the soldier, not once glancing at the woman. He had been an officer in Vlasov's army,[8] the son of old émigrés from France. It surprised me that he hadn't bothered to change his military uniform.

Returning home, I was troubled for a long time by thoughts of how Russians treated other Russians.

"So why am I a Soviet and not a Russian?" I asked myself. Indeed, all my ancestors, except my maternal grandmother and some distant Polish ancestors on my father's side, had been Russians. I wondered if it was really true that nationality changed with the change of a political system, for this was not the first time I had experienced such treatment. In the transit camp in Poznan, the Poles resented my daughter and me only because of political alliances beyond our control. My native land was Russia, and I was Russian; however, Polish hatred for the Soviet government, coupled with a narrow-mindedness and unwillingness to understand the difference between the people and the system of government, caused us much pain.

Nevertheless, we were later able to find devoted friends, advisors, and helpers in our misfortune among the refugees of the first emigration. We were helped by kind people of other nationalities as well.

Thanks to an American military doctor whose name, to my great regret, I do not remember, my daughter began to recover from her bout with scrofula. When we were liberated from the farm, Anechka's condition had grown worse. I knew the only way to save her was to find an American doctor. Holding her in my arms, I set off to where a military unit was located.

I approached the sentry and spoke to him in German. He didn't comprehend a word I was saying, so I tried Russian. This didn't help either, and he simply responded, with a smile, that he didn't understand me.

Just then, a jeep drove up and stopped so that one of its passengers could ask the sentry something. I showed the passenger my daughter's head and said "doctor." Fortunately, the word is similar in English and Russian: after the officer looked at Anechka, he took us to a medical unit without another word.

After an examination and some questions, which I could not answer, they brought me a bottle of cod-liver oil and some tablets. This medicine took effect, and after a while scabs began to fall off the affected areas on her head.

I will always remember the kindness of these soldiers. At last my daughter's condition was improving. She could sleep normally and became animated and lively. She began to chatter all the time, even though she still couldn't pronounce the letter r. Seeing her improve so dramatically made her speech seem all the more charming to me.

One June day, I rose early so that I could finish a job for a customer. I had to alter a man's suit, and it was a difficult task for an inexperienced seamstress. While playing in the street with the other children, my daughter often heard how the fathers of some of her friends had returned from captivity. Thoughts began to stir in her head that her father also would come home.

"Where is my papa?" she asked me one day very seriously. "Why hasn't he come? I want to have a papa, too!"

My little child! What was left for me to say to her, if not the real truth?

"Your papa will never come," I had to tell her. "He is dead, but you have a mama who loves you."

"Yes, but why did the other children not have papas and now they do?" she insisted.

Apparently, the notion of death was incomprehensible to her. Seeing the tears in my eyes, she held out her arms, hugged me around the neck, and began to wipe my tears away with her hands.

"Don't cry, Mamochka! Don't cry, don't cry!"

I began to smile and set her on the floor, and she ran outside again.

We had enough food, so I was even able to help others in need. I helped many secure a place in these unfinished little houses. My sewing work distracted me from distressing thoughts of the future. It was necessary to live only one day at a time. The Treaty of Yalta hung over our heads like a heavy hammer. Many of the refugees did not understand the significance of this agreement and did not realize that America was fulfilling the agreement to which it was bound. The refugees did not want to believe that a democratic country was applying force and was giving us back into the jaws of the bloodthirsty monster. This thought never left me for a minute. Although we continued to live in the house, we were registered to a Russian camp.

The days were monotonous and without much joy. One such day I was about to bring Anechka inside to feed her lunch and have her take a nap afterward. I was almost at the door when I heard a light knock. I opened the door and saw my daughter accompanied by three men. Two of them were younger, and the third was a little bit older.

"Excuse me . . ." began the older one.

At that very moment my daughter, holding his hand, interrupted him and said to me, "It's not true that my father died! My father was at the war and has come home!"

I blushed terribly, tried to say something, but could not immediately find the appropriate words. The unknown man rescued me.

"Forgive the disturbance!" he said. "While we were walking along the highway, we met your Russian neighbors and asked them where we could stop. They pointed us to

your house and said that you would help us. We have everything we need to boil up some soup," he continued. "We've
already been on the road for a whole month, walking from
Czechoslovakia."

I invited them in. Their appearance was terrible, their
clothing dirty and rumpled, and their faces sunburned and
weary. The face of the older man showed particular fatigue.
The youngest pulled a tin of canned meat and a total of three
small potatoes from a rucksack. This was their "everything"
for soup. I began to prepare lunch and heat water for them
to wash. My neighbors gave them some clothing. They ate
heartily, and their appearance improved after bathing with
soap and changing their clothing.

It was clear that they had fled from the Soviet army's
advance into Czechoslovakia. I asked them who they were
and where they were going. Sensing that they had come
upon a sympathetic woman, they cautiously told their story.

My daughter would not leave the man, whose name
I still did not know, for a second. When an eight-year-old
boy named Goga followed her example and leaned on the
stranger's knee, she immediately pushed his arm away.

"Get away from my papa!" she demanded with a rising voice. "This is my papa; he's come home from the war."

Hearing her say that, I knew that if there had been a
cliff I probably would have leapt off it. I was mortified. I did
not know how to explain to her and to convince her that it
wasn't her father; I just turned crimson.

I went to the old Pole who managed the houses, to
find a place for these new people. He showed me a house on
the edge of the settlement that had no doors, only walls and
a roof. After lunch I took them to the empty house. There
was no stove in the kitchen, but they did not need one, since
they planned to continue their journey westward to the
French zone, where no one was forcefully extradited to the
Soviets.

Anechka followed him all day. When it was her bed-
time, I went out to the street and called her. No one answered. I went to the newcomers' house.

"You wouldn't know where my daughter is?" I asked.
He continued to lounge on his plank bed and only answered

with a smile. "What an ignoramus!" I thought, but he continued to lie there with a crafty smile on his face.

"No, she's not here," he said, indicating with a motion of his hand that she was lying behind his back.

I walked over and saw how she pressed tightly to his
back, hiding from me.

"I don't want to go home—I'm going to sleep with
my papa!" she begged tearfully.

"You can come here in the morning. He will be here,"
I tried to persuade her.

Finally, this man had to carry Anechka back to our
house. From the first meeting, there was love at first sight
between "father" and "daughter." Intuition told my daughter that this man would be a good and loving father.

I got to know this gentleman, whose name was Ivan
Nikolaevich, better. He told me about himself, about how he
loved Russian history and reading books of legendary Russian commanders' heroic exploits. He possessed a sharp
mind. When he graduated from the institute, he was taken
into the army and sent to officers' school. Like thousands of
victims of Stalinist terror and purges, Ivan Nikolaevich was
arrested in the Marshal Tukhachevskii affair, and sentenced
by a military tribunal to be shot.[9]

Ivan Nikolaevich was placed in solitary confinement
for 109 days, expecting to be shot at any moment. During
that period his hair turned completely gray and then fell out.

On the last day of his confinement, a man in an NKVD
uniform came into his cell and pulled a paper out of his sleeve
that said that Ivan Nikolaevich's death sentence had been
commuted to twenty-five years' imprisonment.

"The Soviet government has taken your youth into
account," the NKVD agent emphasized.

Ivan Nikolaevich was driven on foot, with other political prisoners, to build a railroad in the Karelskaia region.
Many of his fellow prisoners died during this trip. They
would try to help each other keep moving, since the guards
shot anyone who fell down. The prisoners were fed almost
nothing on the road.

When they were herded into one transit camp, Ivan
Nikolaevich met his former senior officer, who had also been

arrested in the Tukhachevskii affair. This man, however, had been lucky—he worked in the kitchen. The meeting was joyful, even under such conditions. He fed Ivan Nikolaevich pearl-barley kasha, which proved to be too much for his food-deprived system, and Ivan Nikolaevich almost died from twisted bowels. He survived, though, and was eventually sent to the Marinskii camp, where he continued to serve his sentence until the start of the war, in 1941.

When the German troops destroyed the first line of Soviet defense and began to invade the depths of the country with lightning speed, Stalin, "the wise leader," realized that he had decapitated the army, exterminated the best officers, and sent the remainder to labor camps. Those who had survived were immediately summoned to the commandant's office, issued a military uniform, and dispatched to rest homes where they could recuperate before being sent to battle.

Ivan Nikolaevich told me about a dream he had before this event: as he was walking out of his barracks, he saw the rising sun before him. The barbed wire and the machine gun towers had vanished, and there was not another soul to be seen. He saw a road before him that stretched far ahead to the horizon, and he began to run down that road.

At that moment, Ivan Nikolaevich had awakened from his dream. The next morning, he was called into the commandant's office and informed, "Judgment was passed on you by enemies of the people; they have already all been executed. Your country knows that no guilt is ascribed to you."

So began a new epic in Ivan Nikolaevich's life. He was restored to his former rank and sent to the rest home for an entire month. It was there that the prisoners learned of Hitler's attack on our homeland. He was sent to the most dangerous places on the front—mine fields—from which there was often no return.

He loved his troops, and when he saw the dead on the field of battle he cried openly. Having already forgotten all the insults, degradations, and interrogations he had suffered during his trial and imprisonment, he honorably fulfilled his duty to the Motherland—but not to the Communist Party or its leader. While he never considered treason or treachery, one incident turned his thoughts in another direction.

The Soviets had successfully repulsed the Germans' bridgehead near Leningrad at the Kronshtadt fortifications, and thousands of Germans had been taken prisoner. Since the success of the mission was due to their learning the secret password from four German soldiers captured before the attack and the fortifications were now under Soviet control, there was no need for Ivan Nikolaevich's troops to use either the preparatory aerial bombardment or artillery fire as they advanced.

Before the dispatch with this information reached the main headquarters, however, Ivan Nikolaevich was sentenced to be shot for failure to obey the high command's orders. Thus, for the second time in his life, this innocent man had been sentenced to death. Of course, when they learned of the capture of the fortifications, the death sentence was immediately changed. As a former prisoner, however, he was on the blacklist anyway.

After the successful capture of the fortifications, the order came for all the adjoining units to assemble at an open place to watch the execution of "cowards and deserters." The squadrons formed, and several soldiers were marched before them. Ivan Nikolaevich was standing near the place of execution and could hear the voices of those condemned to death. One of the soldiers, no more than seventeen years old, was only guilty of not obeying his commander's order to leap from the trench and attack under enemy fire. This young soldier dropped to his knees and began to implore forgiveness.

"Oh, *diaden'ki*,[10] I want to live, I will do whatever you tell me," he begged for mercy, sobbing.

The form of address bespoke the fact that he had only recently been taken from some village, completely unprepared for battle. It was only natural that his fear for his life overwhelmed his duties.

"When I heard his sobs and supplication, I realized that this was no soldier, but a boy," Ivan Nikolaevich told me. "I could not endure this. I wanted to shoot those who had given such an order."

Fourteen soldiers were executed in this "parade of Soviet unity." Moreover, the bungling general who ordered this show did not take into account the danger in which he placed hundreds of troops, as German planes still dominated in the air. They soon discovered the concentration of troops and dropped bombs and poured machine gun fire down upon them. How many perished because of this attack was known only to the command, not to the soldiers.

This event inspired a change in Ivan Nikolaevich's thinking. Even before this tragedy, he had understood that the Soviet government did not place a high value on the lives of its people or soldiers. To the Party and its leaders, a dead man or a squashed fly were the same. Yet Ivan Nikolaevich knew that there was no other way out except through fulfilling his duties, regardless of his thinking.

Ivan Nikolaevich was to be sent to a new breach to form a parachute brigade, not far from the main railroad station. The station manager, an informant, reported the formation to the Germans. When the parachute brigade launched the assault force, they were met with a continuous hurricane of fire from the ground. Nearly all of them perished. Ivan Nikolaevich was seriously wounded and fell prisoner to the Germans. In accordance with Soviet military regulations, he had tried to shoot himself upon landing, before being taken prisoner, but on the ground four German soldiers jumped at him and pulled the pistol from his fingers, although with difficulty.

"So I was out of Soviet prison and now in German captivity!" he told me. "Is this possible?"

Both his legs had been shot through many times, but he was interrogated by the Germans anyway. He was completely silent through four days of interrogations. He had no food. Only when he met his former senior officer, who had also been taken prisoner, did he begin to eat.

Any officer or soldier who fell prisoner was in a difficult situation. In accordance with Soviet military doctrine, those who were captured were considered traitors to the homeland, a treachery for which there was only one punishment: the firing squad. "The last bullet is for yourself," stated the Soviet regulations. A man had to shoot himself before being taken prisoner. Ivan Nikolaevich had tried but was unsuccessful. What a fate!

The Treaty of Yalta, our own spies and traitors, the unfriendly and in some cases hostile attitudes of those from the first emigration—none of these conditions promised a joyful outcome in the search for salvation. When Ivan Nikolaevich came to us, he had intended to move on, although he himself did not know his destination. Meeting my daughter and me stopped him. He registered himself at the camp and began to take an active part in the defense of our refugees.

Each morning as I awoke, I would think of him, fearing that perhaps he had gone away and that I would never see him again. I hurried to make coffee to take to the small house where he and the others lived. Opening the door, I would be filled with joy—he was always there. Usually with a cigarette in his hand, he would jump up from his chair with a smile on his face and thank me. Coffee in those days was a scarce commodity and almost impossible to obtain, but I didn't know that Ivan Nikolaevich and his companions disliked coffee. They never drank it and poured it out a window after I had gone.

Exchanging outlooks and remembering our own pasts, Ivan Nikolaevich and I understood each other. We had a common view of the past, and we often discussed the future. Ivan Nikolaevich was a great optimist and believed deeply in a bright future for our nation. I often contradicted him in this respect. I am not a pessimist, but I look at reality without illusions.

The continual danger of our existence, coupled by our similar philosophies, brought Ivan Nikolaevich and me closer together and led to our decision to unite our lives and share a common fate. He and I found in each other a stronghold and strength. One evening, I went to fetch my daughter and get her ready for bed. Ivan Nikolaevich invited me to come in and talk seriously about the future. We could not tell what the future might bring us, but we knew that we had to establish ourselves somehow and lighten our burdens. In June 1945, we registered at the German registrar's office as husband and wife, although we did not have a church wedding.

My little daughter had played a great role in uniting our lives. Later, he told me that he had been married with two children—a son and a daughter. All his family had perished during the bombings. He said his little girl had looked very much like my Anechka, which was apparently the main reason for his immediate attachment to her.

Ivan Nikolaevich was an educated and well-read man. He adored nature and animals, especially dogs and horses. He could never pass by small children without a smile expressing his boundless love for them. I admired the depth of his knowledge, his strong character, and his tenacity of spirit, but at times he was also an intolerable man. Often, when making demands of me, he used coarse language, which I was unable to accept for a long time.

My daughter found herself a father, and her mother, a husband. If before this time I had worried for my child's life, now I felt increased anxiety for Ivan Nikolaevich's life—and not without cause.

4

Ivan Nikolaevich lived with Anechka and me in a former school club in which bunkbeds had been set up. The walls separating the families were simple blankets hung between the bunkbeds, and tables stood in the middle of the room. No one complained of the crowding and discomfort.

On day in 1945, four people arrived at our settlement. Before my time in Germany, I had known two of them well, a man and wife. The man, Denisov, was now very ill. I prepared easily digestible food for him and provided as much support as possible. Later, however, I could tell by listening to his wife's conversations that she sympathized with the Soviets. She even began to tell people's fortunes from a deck of cards, saying to some of the nonreturnees, "There is a long road before you. You are afraid, but this is all unnecessary. A happy, joyful life awaits you." Under his wife's influence, Denisov also began to change his political views noticeably.

Seeing all this, I gradually distanced myself from

them. It was difficult for me to understand how they could change their colors so quickly, just like chameleons. Denisov had served in a German unit, retreated with the Germans, but now had changed his tune. We did not suspect their connection with the Soviet Repatriation Mission at first.

Following instructions from the representatives of the Soviet Repatriation Mission, this couple began to propagate slander about nonreturnees who were confirmed anti-Communists. They recruited a group of unscrupulous people, but their actions became obvious to the rest of us. Soon their only option was to move to the Soviet Repatriation Mission's building. Owing to our trust in them when they had first arrived, the pair knew that both Ivan Nikolaevich and I were staunch anti-Communists. It goes without saying that they reported to the Soviet officers our sentiments and those of many other nonreturnees.

By the beginning of August 1945, representatives of the Soviet Repatriation Mission were allowed to examine the card index with the names of the so-called new émigrés (who were still considered Soviet subjects). The general, who was in charge of the camp, wanted to be rid of the "Soviet scum"—as some members of the first emigration referred to those of the second. Hating the Soviet government, the first émigrés transferred their enmity to us. Soviet officers began to summon all those who had been registered as Soviet citizens for interviews. I don't believe their interrogations were wholly successful, because people simply did not show up for them.

One time Soviet officers, one of them a translator, visited a refugee camp in the English zone and brought an old Russian woman to the English officer. Like so many others, all of her family had perished in a Soviet concentration camp. She and a male cousin had been evacuated and eventually ended up in Germany. Throwing herself to her knees before the English officer, she begged, "Little son, don't send me away, I still want to live! I lost my whole family in the homeland!"

"What is she saying?" the English officer asked the Soviet translator.

"She is asking that you must return her to her homeland as quickly as possible!" the Soviet officer "translated" without shame or conscience. Turning to the old woman he said in Russian, "It's good everywhere that we're not, old woman."

"And I want to live where you are not!" cried the old woman.

The English officer, believing the translator's words, promised to send her to her homeland at the first available opportunity.

Another time, in the village of Murnau, where there was a camp housing Russian, Ukrainian, Polish, and Byelorussian nonreturnees, a representative of the Soviet Repatriation Mission addressed a meeting with words of persuasion: "Return, comrades; the Motherland awaits you."

"The Motherland is our mother, but the father is a son of a bitch!" was the piercing response of an old woman. An explosion of laughter followed.

A Soviet driver parked near the camp during the examination of the card index even told Ivan Nikolaevich what awaited those who were extradited back to their homeland. Ivan Nikolaevich asked Denisov, "Where do you intend to go, you fool? Don't you know what awaits you? Even one of the *sovetchiki* told me that death awaits all of us there."[11]

This man must have dutifully reported Ivan Nikolaevich's comments to the senior Soviet officer. When the first list of refugees to be extradited to the Soviet Union was delivered, Ivan Nikolaevich's name was among the first hundred names.

The secretary to the head of the camp, also from the first emigration, had sympathy for our plight. Without the director knowing, she came to us at night and forewarned Ivan Nikolaevich of his pending extradition. At dawn he left us, deciding to hide somewhere a little farther from the camp. As he walked along, automobiles drove by him, going in different directions. He did not suspect that he was being followed by the Soviet representatives.

When he was far from the city, an automobile suddenly screeched to a halt, and Soviet officers leapt out from all four doors. He saw Denisov in the car and knew who had told the Soviets of his escape. "That's him!" Denisov shouted.

"We would like you to get into the car with us," the senior officer addressed Ivan Nikolaevich.

"I will not sit with you murderers and bloodsuckers," he responded. "If you have the authority to arrest me on territory occupied by the Americans, then I agree to go only to the American commandant, but not to your mission."

The automobile turned around. The driver sat behind the wheel, and Denisov sat in the rear seat. The remaining officers, having surrounded Ivan Nikolaevich, followed on foot.

People began to gather along the edges of the road. Ivan Nikolaevich, not falling silent, loudly told the onlookers all that was seething in his heart: of the terror, lies, and violence of the Soviet government, of the millions of victims, and of the deception of our people by the Communist Party and the government.

The Soviets walked in silence, heads lowered, and listened to this cry of an aching heart. If there was still a hidden spark of justice in them, then they knew that he spoke the truth. The *sovetchiki* themselves were only the executors of the Stalinist mockery of our defenseless people, not the originators of policy.

They agreed to go to the American commandant's office, but the American commander was more on the side of the Soviet officials than on that of the refugees. With his hope for protection having faded, Ivan Nikolaevich realized that he had to look for a new way. In the presence of the commandant, he declared that he agreed to return to his homeland. The American rejoiced and congratulated him on his correct decision. They took him to the Soviet mission and put him in a separate room.

The Soviet officers spoke to him ingratiatingly. "We need people like you. The Motherland lost many command personnel in the war," the liars babbled.

"And how many innocent command personnel did the Motherland lose during the Stalinist purges?" Ivan Nikolaevich thought to himself. "You are silent about that! I know what you need me for . . . so you can put a bullet in the back of my head! That's what you need me for!"

He spent the whole night deep in thought. He had to consider what needed to be done to wrest himself from the enemy's bloody claws. In the morning he was invited to breakfast, where he was to meet with Denisov and his wife. Not wanting to see these villains, Ivan Nikolaevich pleaded a lack of appetite and declined.

"I have a suggestion," said Ivan Nikolaevich. "Give me an accompanying officer, so that I can go to the camp. A young fellow, whom I saved from death before the capitulation, is waiting for me there as well as an eighty-year-old woman."

The woman he referred to had nothing to do with Ivan Nikolaevich, for she lived with her daughter-in-law and grandsons. So that his story would sound more convincing, Ivan Nikolaevich had "registered" her as a member of his family. He deliberately did not mention me or Anechka, since he did not want us pursued, but Denisov had already told them everything about him and me.

"What's with you, comrade? We trust you and know that you will return, especially as you have no other recourse," the senior officer replied agreeably. "You gave your word before the American commandant. Go and bring back the others, and everything will be in order."

Ivan Nikolaevich left the building and set off for the school where we lived, located not far from the mission. Meanwhile I didn't know he had been detained by officers of the Soviet Repatriation Mission.

The American military planners, fulfilling the Yalta agreements, tried to force extradition of former Soviet citizens back to the USSR. The overwhelming resistance, however, led to "Bloody Sunday," surely one of the darkest pages in American military history. On August 9, 1945, large military trucks drove up and American troops surrounded our camp in Kempten. Residents, led by a priest, locked themselves in a huge room at the end of a long corridor in a church. The first company of American soldiers refused to dispatch the refugees by force. The leading officer ordered an encirclement and then withdrew with the soldiers, to avoid the use of force. After a short time more soldiers came and again surrounded the camp. The armed soldiers were able to break the metal doors only with great difficulty. They were met by the priest, holding a cross in his raised hand. A soldier struck at the cross with his rifle butt, which cut the priest's face quite badly.

The people inside the church, most of whom were women and children, raised a terrible outcry. The executors of the Treaty of Yalta began to seize women, knocking them off their feet, dragging them by their legs down the long corridor to the exit, and throwing them into the trucks like sticks of wood.

Someone unsuccessfully tried to hang black flags, a sign of death, from a second-story window. The soldiers tore them away and threw them out the window. One American soldier, outraged by the violence, threw his rifle to the floor, tearfully cried out something in English, and helped to hang out a black flag. Nonreturnees from the Pribaltic states, living in a neighboring camp, helped rescue people by catching them in outstretched blankets as they leapt from the second floor. Some inhabitants of our camp committed suicide by cutting their wrists or taking poison, to avoid falling into the hands of the executioners alive.

The local German population witnessed this violence. The streets were full of people, often voicing Roosevelt's name. "How could he have agreed to this?" could be heard among the spectators.

When this bloodbath began, my daughter and I were in a building adjacent to the camp. I thank God that we were not surrounded by soldiers and were able to hide in the mass of onlookers on the street. Swarms of questions ran through my head. "What shall we do? Where can we run and whom can we ask for help?" After all, our last hope—the Allied protection—had been destroyed. The only barrier that remained between the Soviet Union and us was Germany, a conquered, divided country. The Germans had needed us only when they had lived off our labor; now they could not even provide shelter for their homeless.

In order to hide from pursuit, Anechka and I and a few others fled into the hills on Bloody Sunday. We lived in the mountains beneath the open sky and the pouring rain, without food or proper clothing. We slept fitfully beneath trees on the wet ground, listening intently to every noise, in fear of being found.

Our group was comprised of many people: an ethnic Russian teacher, a family of Byelorussians, and several Ukrainians. We shared everything that we could.

My little daughter, never having completely recovered, became seriously ill once again. I knew I had to do something to save her from death, so I decided to go to a farm to ask for shelter, even if only in a barn. The first two attempts ended unsuccessfully, for the farmers would not talk to me. They were afraid of robberies and looked on foreigners with contempt. When I returned to the group, I could sense alienation and aloofness. The old Ukrainian woman came up to me and said, "I won't be your nanny when you go off someplace."

"I only went to find a place under some roof," I replied. "You can see for yourself that Anechka is quite sick!"

"That doesn't matter to me. I won't help you anymore!" she answered sharply.

Something had occurred in my absence. Surprised at her attitude, I asked her why she now treated me so badly. She only answered with cold silence.

I quietly took my daughter in my arms, moved away from the group, and sat beneath a tree. A lump squeezed my throat, and tears flowed down my cheeks. I felt completely helpless. It seemed as if those I had thought were united with me had turned against me. I wanted to know what exactly had happened and decided to go to the young teacher.

At first he was silent, but then he finally asked me dryly, "What do you want to talk about?"

"Tell me, please, what happened while I was gone? Why is there such hostility toward me all of a sudden?"

"I think you must know why!"

"I don't understand. You are hinting at something. Tell me frankly, please."

"You went to the *sovetchiki*. You're a Soviet agent," he accused. "That's what the woman who came while you weren't here told us."

I was dumbfounded. "Who was this woman?" I asked him. "Where is she? Do you know her?"

"No, but she spoke convincingly of you, that you are a Soviet spy."

"You are a rational, intelligent man," I said in tears. "Would I sit here with you, with a sick child, if I were a spy, as you call me?"

"You should be thankful that I didn't give my pistol to that Cossack," he replied, indicating a man sitting in the distance. "He wanted to lie in wait for you and shoot you when you returned here. I hesitated, but didn't give him the pistol. You see how maliciously he looks at you?"

This slander made it clear that the Soviet method of lies and filth was at work. The visitor had been none other than Denisov's wife, and she successfully recruited the Ukrainian woman from our group, luring her with promises of bountiful gardens of cucumbers and potatoes at her home in Poltava.

Although I was able to convince the others of my hatred for the Soviets, I did not want to remain with the group, since I could not trust them. It was unpleasant to live among such weak, wavering people. Even though my child was sick and had a fever, we had to leave.

I went up to a clearing at the top of a hill. Before me spread a flat meadow. In the distance, by the woods, I saw a house and several large barns. Praying to God, I set off toward the house. As I approached, I noticed that someone quickly stepped away from the window. I knocked and waited. There was no answer, so I knocked again.

The door opened halfway, and a man asked in German with a Bavarian accent what I wanted. I explained my situation while a woman stood quietly behind him. The man was ready to refuse my request when the lady of the house broke into the conversation.

"Are you hungry?" she asked.

"Yes, we have eaten nothing for two days now," I answered.

"Come in, I'll feed you."

The man stepped away from the door, and we entered the room. At first they were quiet and then cautiously began to ask me questions. I discovered that the same woman who had maligned me before the group had also been here on the farm looking for a young woman with a small child. She had described my outward appearance quite accurately, even indicating that I wore a watch on my wrist and a ring on my finger. I explained to them why this woman was searching for me.

These kind people took pity on my plight and offered me a place in one of the barns. The man put straw in a corner and brought a blanket and pillow for us.

By that night, my daughter was burning with fever. I periodically wet a towel in cold water and laid it on her little head. My heart broke, seeing how helpless I was to ease her suffering. How much sorrow and torment had this tiny creature shared with me? She was always calm, never demanded anything of me, as if understanding our despair with her small heart.

Early the next morning, I shared my grief with the lady of the house. She brought us some kind of medicine. My daughter's temperature soon dropped noticeably.

Her first question when she began to get better was "Where is my papa?" referring to Ivan Nikolaevich.

"I don't know, little one," I answered. "Let us hope that he is healthy and that God will preserve him."

CHAPTER SIX

FREEDOM FOUND

1

When I returned to the building where we had lived before Bloody Sunday, I saw a young man, named Peter, lying on the bed. This was the man whose life Ivan Nikolaevich had saved: Ivan Nikolaevich had told the Soviet authorities he would bring him back to the mission. He quickly got up from the bed and addressed me rudely: "What do you want? Go away from here! You're a Soviet spy!"

"My God! Peter!" I exclaimed. "You've lost your mind! Where did you get such nonsense?" I tried to convince him of the absurdity of his accusation.

"Ivan Nikolaevich knows it, too," he continued. "It would be better if he never laid eyes on you again."

After long persuasion, his tone became milder. He finally agreed to take me to the mountains where Ivan Nikolaevich was hiding.

Along the way, Peter told me how they had fled. After Ivan Nikolaevich left the Soviet Repatriation Mission, he returned to the camp. Running into the living quarters, he only had time to shout, "Petia! Quickly! We must flee!"

The two men jumped out the lavatory window and into the garden. They scaled the garden fence and landed in the back street, where a Soviet car was already waiting for them. An ambush had been laid for them.

Instead of stopping them, the Soviet driver only said, "Save yourself, comrade!" They saw it was the same driver who earlier had told Ivan Nikolaevich what lay in store for those who were extradited to the Soviet Union. Was it kindness or fear of a confrontation that guided the driver's actions?

Ivan Nikolaevich and Peter made their way to the nearest hills on roundabout roads and hid in a marshy area overgrown with tall green ferns. En route to this place, they were followed by a bicyclist dressed in Tyrolean clothing. They managed to lose him eventually.

Two weeks had passed since Ivan Nikolaevich and I parted, and we knew nothing of what happened to each other. Now I was on my way to him with Peter, who scowled at me the whole time. Nearing the place where Ivan Nikolaevich was hiding, Peter suddenly turned to me and said, "I want to search you . . . you may be carrying a pistol."

"You idiot, you still don't trust me. Go ahead! Search!" I was wearing a suit, and he felt under the jacket. I had never in all my life fired or learned to use a pistol, although I had been taught to break down and reassemble a rifle in a school course on military preparedness.

We climbed a high hill covered with tall trees. Peter told me authoritatively to wait and disappeared. A little while later he returned and sternly commanded me to follow.

The descent from the hill was very steep, so all I could do was slide down. At the bottom of the hill, Ivan Nikolaevich stood on the edge of the marsh. Exhausted, but with a smile, he awaited me. Taking me into his arms, he repeated, "How can I forgive you, how can I forgive you?"

"Forgive what?" I asked him. "You know that this is the slander of the *sovetchiki*, with the help of Denisov and his wife."

Peter had brought bread and canned meat, which we ate together. Realizing that the bicyclist knew approximately where we might be, and knowing that the *sovetchiki* would be searching this area, we had to move to a new hiding place. Peter returned to camp, and Ivan Nikolaevich and I began to make our way to my refuge. It was a considerable distance away, so we arrived at the barn late in the evening.

The next morning, I returned to the city to see my daughter, whom I had temporarily left with a Russian friend named Marfa Timofeevna. She and her family lived in a private apartment, and the *sovetchiki* had not yet managed to

reach them. My daughter was in safe hands, but I nevertheless worried about her. Ivan Nikolaevich and I agreed that
he would wait for me in the bushes not far from where the
hills began to rise, until nine o'clock in the evening. If I wasn't
there by nine o'clock, it meant that the *sovetchiki* had detained
me and that he should hide elsewhere.

I stayed in the city until it began to get dark. Carrying
a small sack of food, I began my return trip near a deep
ravine. In order to avoid the open road, I descended into the
ravine, making my way with difficulty through the dense
brush. The road ran through the forest and climbed up into
the mountains.

I had just entered the forest and breathed a sigh of
relief when I heard a quiet conversation (I could not tell in
what language) and a rustling in the bushes. My legs began
to tremble, and I began to stumble. My whole body was frozen with fright. On one side of the road was a deep drop and
the sound of splashing water. Gasping for air, I continued
up the mountain and made my way to our refuge and then
to the bushes where Ivan Nikolaevich was to wait for me.

Our rendezvous was to take place in a clearing near
the road. As I came out of the woods, I noticed four silhou-
ettes beneath a tree. Apparently the four did not immediately
see me, because I was in dark clothing against the shadowy
background of the woods. Suddenly all four of them dropped
to the ground. I then realized that they were waiting for me.

The ambush was at a site where I could not jump over
the edge of the steep overhang on one side of the road. A
marsh, encircled by barbed wire, lay on the other side of the
road. I surveyed the situation and saw that my only means
of escape lay in squeezing through the barbed wire. Thoughts
of despair swirled in my head. It seemed as though my life
had reached its end. I knew that if the first men in the ambush
let me through, the second ones would catch me.

I picked my way through the huge coils of barbed
wire, my heart beating so violently that it seemed ready to
burst from my chest. The sharp and rusty barbs tore my clothing and scratched my arms and legs, drawing blood. During
this effort, however, I felt as though some force lifted my

spirits and drove me on. With great difficulty, I passed through the wire.

The edge of the marsh extended into a distant clearing where farmers deposited liquid manure during the day. It was not possible to walk through this clearing, so I had to crawl on my hands and knees. Feeling no pain in my hands or legs, I sneaked up to our refuge in the barn and listened. Silence. I entered the barn. No one. Now I began to worry about Ivan Nikolaevich. What had happened to him? I had on my wrist a watch with a glowing dial and saw that it was already eleven-thirty. I went out of the barn and sat down, peering into the darkness and listening to the sounds of the night birds and the light footfalls of the mountain creatures.

I could not think of what to do next. My child was in the city, and Ivan Nikolaevich was somewhere in the bushes. Only God alone knew whether or not he was alive.

At one o'clock, I heard a rustle in the grass and someone's light steps. Looking into the distance, I could see no one, but the noise kept coming closer. Finally I saw the silhouette of a man creeping up to the barn. Who was it? Perhaps a *sovetchik*?

Finally, I recognized Ivan Nikolaevich and quietly called to him. He quickened his pace and hurled himself at me, telling me that he had lost hope of seeing me. He had not been far from the planned ambush and even had heard Russian spoken, though not all the words were clear. He had heard their cursing, so it was clear who they were.

We both went into the barn. There was firewood stacked high around our refuge, so we were able—without bringing attention to ourselves—to light the candle given to me by the farmer's wife.

"What's the matter with you?" cried Ivan Nikolaevich. "You're all bloody!" Only then did I feel pain from the wounds which covered my arms, legs, and face. Blood trickled from the cuts and abrasions.

We had to wait for dawn to wash and dress the wounds. In the morning I went to the farmers, who gave me first aid. But it was too late—as infection brought about by the rusty wire and the liquid manure had set in.

It was not possible to remain where we were. Although I was constantly worried about my child, we nevertheless decided to make our way farther into the mountains and to hide in the woods. In the mountains we found dense thickets, where I left Ivan Nikolaevich. With bandaged arms and legs, and wearing a suit torn in many places, I went to see my daughter, who was still staying with Marfa Timofeevna.

Our lives continued in this way for about two months. Ivan Nikolaevich let his beard grow and then decided to shave it off, using water from a puddle. He nicked himself with the razor, and the cuts subsequently became infected. His face was covered with measles-like abscesses.

We knew we could not live under such conditions much longer and that we had to find a way out of the situation. The nights were cold and the days were rainy. We were constantly hungry. During my visits to Marfa Timofeevna, she shared with me her own modest rations, but her own family consisted of seven people.

I decided to turn to the deputy of the director of the camp in Kempten. A Russian engineer from Yugoslavia, he had given me the impression of being a good person who would be sympathetic to our misfortune. While we were in hiding, it had become more peaceful in the camp. Those who had run away either were still in the mountains or had made their way to other camps of nonreturnees, registering themselves as Poles, Yugoslavs, or Czechs—any nationality but Russian. A few passed themselves off as old émigrés.

He heard my story in silence. I told him of all my ordeals before and during the war. He already was aware that Ivan Nikolaevich and a few others had taken up the defense of the new emigrants. The members of this "delegation" had been to see the American commandant several times, but their visits had been futile.

Having heard me out, the engineer Nikitin, took a pen and began to write. He put the sheet of paper in an envelope and held it out to me.

"This is a letter to my good friend Borel. He will help you to get settled in his camp."

It was about fifty kilometers to the camp, located in Zontgofen. I did not dare to go on foot, with the abscesses on my legs. Wounds healed very slowly in Bavaria, particularly when no preventative measures had been taken. The trains went to Zontgofen, but we had no money for tickets. Once again, we found good people who helped us. I went by myself with the letter for Borel.

The camp was located in a hollow between mountains, not far from the border with Switzerland and Austria. Though I had always admired the beauty of mountains and had seen in them a mysterious grandeur, I didn't notice the alpine scenery. I was worn out from my wanderings about the hills and brush surrounding Kempten, and my thoughts were now concentrated on one thing: to survive and not to fall into the tyrant's jaws.

I arrived at Borel's office, but he was away at a meeting. The secretary of the Russian section was a Russian émigré from Yugoslavia. I explained to her that I had a letter for Borel from his friend, the engineer Nikitin. She insisted that I give her the letter, but I refused, saying that I wished to speak to Borel personally and that the fate of my family depended on it. She became quiet, occasionally looking sullenly at me, and continued to type. I sat silently and waited, immersed in painful thoughts.

Borel finally appeared, and the secretary pointed me out to him. He was an imposing man, with very handsome features. He suggested that I enter his office, where I gave him Nikitin's letter. He read it with great attention, then asked how he could help.

Not concealing anything, I revealed to him the whole truth about myself and about Ivan Nikolaevich. While I was telling of my sufferings, of my fear for my daughter's life, he gazed at me intently, not taking his eyes off me.

"You didn't need this letter at all, for I would have helped you even without it," he said solemnly, with sympathy and sorrow etched in his face.

"How much longer will our people suffer?" he asked sadly of no one in particular. "In his letter, Mister Nikitin indicated 'that the bearer of this letter enjoys my full confidence.' What you have said about yourself summons an inescapable belief and sympathy from every true man."

"We are persecuted and defenseless," he continued. "They persecuted us without cause in our homeland. Here they do not all understand us, nor do they want to. We are unwanted people, and we are knocked about like a soccer ball, for Stalin's pleasure. You see what our allies have done with us? To please Stalin, at Yalta they signed the 'death sentence' of us new refugees, that is, the forceful repatriation of all Soviet subjects. The questions arises, 'Why don't these people want to return to their homeland?' It is because the powers of tyranny, violence, and misery have pushed these people to such a step. I promise you my full support and will help you to register in our camp," Borel concluded. "Go back to Kempten and bring your family here."

I was unable to restrain my tears of gratitude. He opened the door and touched me on the shoulder.

"Do you have money for the train?" he asked. A painful silence ensued. I was ashamed to admit that we didn't even have a kopek.

"I see that you don't." He opened a purse and gave me money. "I hope it will be enough."

I wanted to hug and kiss him as a brother, but I felt it would be awkward.

I returned to Kempten late in the evening. My daughter was already asleep. The next morning, as I set off for the forest to get Ivan Nikolaevich, I was pursued relentlessly by fear. I knew I had to fight this feeling.

During the two days of my absence, the infection on Ivan Nikolaevich's face had grown even worse, and he could barely open his mouth. My own wounds were festering, and my legs moved woodenly. My pain was null compared to my feelings of helplessness and fear for the lives of my loved ones.

After telling Ivan Nikolaevich about all that had happened during my trip to Zontgofen, we drew up a plan to get there. We both looked horrible. To cover the sores on his chin and lips, I wrapped his head in a kerchief and knotted it on top. Carrying a small bundle, we set off for the city to fetch Anechka and Peter. Both were happy to see us. The four of us went to the railroad station and bought tickets. While waiting to board, we glanced nervously around, fearing that someone might come up and ask to see our papers.

No one asked to see them, thank God, and we reached Zont-gofen safely.

After we left the train, without a second glance we continued our journey to the camp. Along the way we met a Russian woman from the camp in Kempten. She advised us not to go to this camp. "They aren't registering anyone any-more," she tried to convince us. "Go back to Kempten." We said nothing in reply.

When we arrived at the camp, Borel himself took us to the storehouse, where they issued the refugees blankets and some clothing. We returned to the barracks together. The camp was quite large; the majority of its inhabitants were Poles and Ukrainians from the western Ukraine. The Russian refugees occupied only one of the barracks.

The secretary of the Russian camp summoned a *bloko-voi*,[1] who took us to a second-floor room. There was a bunkbed in the corner of the room; this was considered our apartment. Three elderly Russians, who had been officers of the White Army, were in the room. Like Borel, they had lived in Yugoslavia.

All of us, including Peter, whom we had adopted as a son, went to register at the camp's office, so that we could receive our papers. The director of this main office, a former Polish officer in Anders' army,[2] greeted us affably and invited us to sit down. Borel had apparently told him about us al-ready.

He began to question Ivan Nikolaevich, who an-swered all his questions truthfully. He admitted his Soviet citizenship and told of his confinement in prison and the *kontslager'* and of the horrors of his captivity in Germany. The officer wrote down only what information was required on the forms.

Having finished his interview with Ivan Nikolaevich, he began to question me. I also told everything about myself. The officer regarded me with special sympathy when he learned that my first husband had been a Catholic of Polish ancestry who had been killed by the Germans.

We were heartened by this officer's warmth during the registration process and expressed our deepest thanks as we headed for the door. As I opened the door, we bumped into a Soviet major from Kempten, accompanied by the same lieutenant who had translated for the American commandant in Kempten during Ivan Nikolaevich's interrogation. We didn't know if they recognized Ivan Nikolaevich with his face half wrapped in the kerchief. Once again danger and fear hung over our heads.

Among the residents of the Russian camp was a young man who had served in the Soviet army during the war. He was a kind man, but also very daring. We called him the Corporal. When he told us about himself, we learned that even before the war he had been in many difficult situations, but had always come out unharmed. He had been taken prisoner by the Germans very early in the war and had survived all the horrors of captivity: hunger, cold, hard labor, illnesses. Then, having "emerged the victor," as he said, he decided to choose the road of a nonreturnee. His parents, dispossessed Kulaks, had been exiled to Siberia, where they died.

His entire life thus became driven by hatred of both the Soviet and Fascist tormenters and persecutors. He despised the Soviet government, not only for the destruction of his family, but also for the conditions he had experienced in the army. "They gave a rifle to ten men and said 'fight as you like!' " he said sarcastically of Soviet military preparedness.

Like all of us, however, he loved his homeland and his people. He strove all he could to ease the suffering of others less fortunate than him. He looked like a hooligan, but had a good heart.

Learning of our concern for Ivan Nikolaevich's safety, he suggested that my husband temporarily leave the camp. Ivan Nikolaevich agreed immediately, and together they set off for the mountains, where the Corporal himself had not long ago hidden from Soviet officials.

The day after he had hidden Ivan Nikolaevich, the Corporal asked me if I would like to go with him to the old hunter's cabin where Ivan Nikolaevich was staying.

"After all, he needs food, cigarettes, and other things," the Corporal said.

I agreed without hesitation. Peter stayed with Anechka in the barracks. It was a long way to the cabin. One side of the road was a high ridge with a flat rock wall that not even an experienced mountain climber could scale. We skirted it and began our difficult ascent on its far side, through the rich vegetation. Stopping along the way to catch our breath, we reached the top at last. A beautiful panorama spread before my eyes. I could see mountains in the distance and a valley with meadows and fields below.

"What beauty God created. Why can't everyone enjoy it?" I thought as we approached the hunter's cabin. "Why must there be oppressed and oppressors?" I continued thinking. "Why have they pursued us, and why do they continue to do so? Who can answer these questions?"

We arrived at the small cabin. The Corporal knocked three times, as agreed with Ivan Nikolaevich. The door opened, and the fugitive embraced me. Tears shone in his eyes and he couldn't speak.

"How did you pass the night?" I asked him, breaking the silence.

"Don't ask! This is a horror! I didn't sleep for even a minute. There were cries and footsteps. It seemed to me that at any minute someone would knock on the door."

These noises had not been people, but the calls of night birds and movements of wild animals. My husband's fears were justified, however, because some straggling SS troops, who had not surrendered to the Americans, were still hiding in the mountains.

The Corporal returned to the camp, and I remained with Ivan Nikolaevich. Only then did I understand what he had experienced that first night alone. Although he no longer felt alone and fell asleep early that evening even before his head touched the pillow, I could not close my eyes the whole night, trembling from fear and cold. In the morning we decided that I should return to the camp to find out through Borel and the Polish officer whether we had been recognized by the *sovetchiki*.

Our fears were unfounded, so I once again set off for the mountains and brought Ivan Nikolaevich back to the camp. After our return to the camp, however, we still couldn't find a peaceful existence. The *sovetchiki* visited all the displaced person camps and demanded to inspect the card files listing the Soviet citizens. The *sovetchiki* knew that many of the nonreturnees were masquerading as old émigrés. The inhabitants of the camps often were summoned by a joint American-Soviet commission for questioning.

The Americans began to understand the mistake of Yalta, with regard to the forceful return of refugees, and became more sympathetic to our misfortune. Slowly, American policy shifted in our favor. The Americans no longer told nonreturnees to "go home but don't vote for Stalin." All the same, these were overdue and torturous steps for us in the direction of change.

The path for those who have lost their homeland is cruel and thorny. "A man without a homeland is like a nightingale without a song," according to the old Russian proverb. It was sad to see suffering and grief reflected in my compatriots' faces. We found ourselves at a dead end with no clear exit. Besides the persecution of repatriation, many families had been separated, and the fates of many were unknown. The missing could be alive or dead, killed in German camps, or at hard labor in the mines and factories, or crushed beneath bombed-out buildings.

How many times in my life had I looked death straight in the eye? Seeing all the tragedies of these people and reflecting on my own personal experiences when life was hanging by a hair, I became more and more a deep believer in God. I also grew to believe in fate. While this may sound fatalistic, it is an undeniable underpinning in my philosophy of life.

> What is to be, will be,
> Thus since youth has sung
> The street-organ into the low window.[3]

My nature would not permit me to sit in the camp and "wait for the weather to come from the sea."[4] I had to busy myself with something to dull the keenness of my experiences and alleviate the pain. What could I do in the camp?

Seeing the children of the camp run about, the answer to the question struck me: I would organize a school for the nonreturnees' children. They were losing the best time to learn and acquire knowledge. With the support of Borel, this idea became a reality.

He and I went to the American commandant in Zontgofen, who helped us obtain from German schools things
such as desks and chalkboards. At first, we didn't have
books, notebooks, or pencils, but we gradually acquired what
we needed. We set up three classrooms in a garret. I taught
all the subjects of an elementary school program. I received
no pay for my work, but was issued a worker's ration: a few
chocolate bars, cigarettes, and leftover bread. I didn't work
for rations, however; I instead felt a duty and obligation to
my compatriots, and especially to the rising generation.

This school enabled us to reestablish ties with other
Russian camps. People even began to print school materials
on a rotary press. Refugees from other camps came, and the
number of students increased so much that we needed addi-
tional help. Although there were many former teachers
among the nonreturnees, many feared to admit that they
were from the Soviet Union. One could not blame them for
such cautiousness in hiding their pasts.

In 1946, the United Nations Relief and Rehabilitation
Administration, which at that time was in charge of the refugees, decided for some reason to transfer all Russians, Byelorussians, and some Ukrainians to the small town of Oberammergau. We were settled in housing units that had earlier
been used for workers from the east. The barracks in the
Oberammergau camp had gray concrete walls and floors,
which produced an unbelievable melancholy. School did not
exist in Oberammergau, for there were no provisions for it.
Parents began to demand that lessons resume. Their pressure
on the camp administration was rewarded with success.

The conditions were terrible, but we didn't complain,
as we could breathe easier. The Soviet screenings were conducted more seldom. Rumors still spread that all of us nonreturnees would eventually be sent back to our homeland anyway. Most of these rumors were spread by Soviet agents in
an effort to make the lives of the nonreturnees still more
intolerable. To all the nonreturnees, one thing was clear: no
matter what life brought, it would be better than falling into
the death grip of that supreme demon named Stalin.

Once I dreamed that I was returned to the Soviet
Union and that an NKVDist with a ferocious, inhuman

expression on his face was questioning me: "You fled from Siberia? Where are your parents? Who gave you the right to eat our Soviet bread? Who gave you, the daughter of an enemy of the people, the right to receive an education?"

"God! God! God! Jesus Christ! My faith in the Savior!" I pleaded in tears. "You ruined my family, you destroyed my parents! You confiscated all our property! You murdered innocent people! My father was an honorable and hard-working man who helped anyone in need! He was not an enemy of the people! You are the enemies!" My own scream awoke me with a start. My heart pounded. Realizing that this was just a horrible dream, I crossed myself and thanked God that this was only a nightmare.

The grief left an imprint in my soul then, and it lives with me even to this day. My family says that I still often sob quietly in my sleep.

Our life together in the camp at Oberammergau was short. It was soon decided to move all women with children to the resort city of Kolgrub, where we were placed in a former hotel. The spot was exceptionally clean and orderly, with rugs in the rooms, divans, comfortable beds, and washstands with hot and cold water. We were able to take mud and sulfur baths. Such luxury was unheard of for many of the inhabitants.

I was asked to resume my work at the school. While all the rooms contained two families, I received a separate room with a beautiful view to conduct lessons. After a full schedule of classes, I would take the children on nature excursions. We climbed low hills and admired the beautiful Bavarian sights. My daughter gradually recovered and became a cheerful chatterbox. She loved to walk with me in the meadows, and I always took her with me on the trips with the schoolchildren.

While my daughter and I were in Kolgrub, Ivan Nikolaevich was still living in Oberammergau. He learned to play cards from several Yugoslavian friends. These games were without losses, as no one had any money at the time. It was as if, after the loss of his status, he sought some kind of acute sensation and found it in card play or in fishing in the mountain streams. He frequently disappeared from the house and reappeared only late in the evening, which caused much concern.

He also assumed the duties of a *blokovoi* and therefore could come see us only on Saturdays. My daughter was delighted when her "Papochka" came. They had loved each other from that first day. To Ivan Nikolaevich, she was just like his own daughter. I was touched by their love for each other. Perhaps this also explains why I forgave Ivan Nikolaevich for his actions, although some of them left a permanent scar in my heart. Although I had in fact saved his life and trusted that he would never think of harming me, it turned out later that my trust was misplaced. I found out several years after the fact that during the first years of our lives together Ivan Nikolaevich had been unfaithful to me. He was not a handsome man, but an inexplicable charm and humor attracted the attention of many women, including me.

He appealed to me from the first days we met. Thinking it more comfortable to explain his feelings about me in writing, he had written a letter to me early in our relationship:

Dear Lenochka,

I must leave Kempten, as day and night thoughts of you do not leave me. But do I have the right to hope my feelings are reciprocated, when danger hangs over both of us? I have never in my life experienced such feelings as I do for you. I will keep all our brief meetings and conversations in my heart as long as I live. Thank you for your warmth and help, and that you have given me comfort in such difficult days. The Russian language is rich, but it is hard for me to find the words to express my thoughts. You will be rewarded by the Most High for your sensitive treatment of the suffering. Forgive and farewell, my friend.

Your Ivan Nikolaevich

Reading this letter, I had been filled with joy that I was no longer alone. Once again I was loved and would be able to love. After the loss of my Antok, I never thought I would be able to experience such feelings for anyone, except for his small daughter.

The struggle to deny my thoughts for Ivan Nikolaevich was in vain. Regardless of the fact that in childhood I had been impulsive and hard to please, I was level-headed as an adult, the result of having traveled the path of suffering and deprivation. I had learned to accept the blows that life dealt me, and I bore them without a murmur. If someone like Ivan Nikolaevich came along life's path and promised a better future, I considered it a reward for the difficulties I had endured. Ivan Nikolaevich Dmitriew and I were joined in a church wedding on July 25, 1946.

2

Many refugees were gradually allowed to emigrate to various countries. The first of these lucky people ended up in Belgium to work in the mines. Then Venezuela, Paraguay, the United States, and Canada began to take them. Life in the nonreturnee camps was difficult and humiliating, but everyone was desperate to avoid a life (and very possibly a death) in the Soviet Union.

I had worked diligently at the school in Kolgrub and Lutensee for more than four years, happy to help children acquire an education, when our opportunity to emigrate to Canada came.

A special commission arrived from Canada to recruit labor for the sugar beet fields, and our Russian administrator could select two families of not less than three workers. To make the selection from so many families, the administration decided that whoever registered first would be able to apply to the Canadian commission. A family of Byelorussians was first on the list. The representative of another family and I arrived at the emigration office at exactly the same time to register for the other slot. The woman working in the department took two matches, broke one in half, but left the other long. She held both matches in her hand and decided that whoever pulled the long match would be registered. I turned out to be the lucky one. The man looked at me with a disappointed expression and only said, "This means it wasn't my fate."

A few days later we were summoned to the Canadian consulate in Munich. After doctors examined us and American intelligence people interviewed us, we went to the consul. The wait took up to three weeks. They sent us back to the camp and said that they would call us when our turn came.

A month went by with no call. I decided to go to Munich myself to find out if anything had happened to our application or whether they had simply forgotten us. All our documents had been approved by the various commissions, and other families had already completed the entire procedure and were waiting to be sent off on the steamer. I arrived in Munich and went directly to the Canadian consul. Realizing I might not find anyone in a single day who could answer my questions, I had to find a place to stay overnight.

While leaving the consulate, I ran into a woman who looked very familiar to me, but I could not immediately remember where I had seen her. She also looked intently at me and spoke first. "I know you from somewhere, but I can't think of how and when I met you." I echoed these words.

We continued our conversation. As it turned out, she was a German language instructor, and I had briefly met her once at a conference before this chance encounter. I told her of my difficulties.

"I think I can help you," she said. "I work as a translator at the Canadian consulate." She spoke perfect German, English, and French. She was of German ancestry but had been born in Russia and had lived there until the war. Wasn't this fate! If I hadn't met her, we would not have been able to reach Canada.

She found our packet of documents, which had been thrown aside for no apparent reason. Officials often moved up the documents of those who could pay bribes. Applications of poor people like us were ignored. "The tsar pities, but not the huntsman," goes the old Russian saying. The consul, of course, was not aware of what happened behind the scene. My new friend arranged a meeting three days later, at the Canadian consul's office.

When I returned to the camp, the family of Byelorussians was already on the way to Bremerhaven, where they were to board a steamer. We quickly gathered our few belongings and set off for Munich. We were immediately received by the consul, who, after an interview, congratulated us and wished us happiness in our new country.

We were quickly placed on a train and were on our way to our ship, the *Samaria*. It was April when we made our crossing, and the ocean was not friendly. Waves lashed the creaking and groaning English steamer, and it even occurred to me that the ship was so old that it might sink. Although there were people of many nationalities on the steamer, you could count the Russians with your fingers. The majority of the passengers were Ukrainians, Poles, and Jews.

From the first day, I was so seasick that I could not eat or even stand. I was terribly ill during nine of the thirteen days it took to cross the ocean. Each morning, Ivan Nikolaevich carried me out to the deck, where I would lie until nearly evening. My little daughter stayed close to me and only when they both went to the dining hall was I left alone.

There are people who worship the ocean, but I am not one of them. To me the ocean has always seemed to have an element of wickedness. With its awesome power, it can easily swallow and bury in its depths everything that struggles feebly. So I was very glad when we reached Canada.

Relatives and friends were at the pier waiting for many of the passengers, but there was no one to meet us or to offer an encouraging word. We felt our solitude all the more. The Canadian officials, only fulfilling their duty, were polite but cold. I was so uncomfortable and fearful of the unknown that I burst into tears and could not calm myself. We had just arrived in a new country that had unfamiliar customs and a foreign language, and we had no idea what our destiny would be.

Nevertheless, we could not criticize the Canadians' treatment of the refugees. We were taken by buses to rest in a village where they gave us very good rooms with clean beds and exceptionally good food. Interpreters who spoke various languages were available. Seeing such friendliness, my heart grew lighter. Only when they took us to Montreal did we feel hostility, especially in a restaurant and at the train terminal. Strangers threw stones at the train, which was to take us to Manitoba. We didn't know who organized this inhospitable behavior, but it left an unpleasant impression that has endured to this day.

I will never forget the day of our train's arrival in Winnipeg on May 5, 1949. Large snowdrifts, covered with mud and just beginning to melt, lay in many places. The wind seemed as though it came directly from Siberia. Our decrepit clothing did nothing to protect us from its biting cold.

Representatives of the Manitoba Parliament's Department of Agriculture met the group of people who intended to work in the sugar beet fields. The minister of this department was a very nice man who, with a smile, tried to converse with all the arrivals, assisted by a translator who spoke German and Russian. The translator had been born in Canada after his parents had left Russia during the Revolution. He felt a brotherly kinship, which was reflected in his graciousness.

My daughter attracted the minister's attention, and he tried to speak with her. Their conversation was short, of course, but we learned from the translator that the minister wished to show us the city. Apparently he liked children very much, for all his attention was concentrated on my Anechka. I still remember that when we crossed a bridge over a river, he told her its name: Red River.

After a short walk around the city, we returned to the station, where we were to await a farmer from Homewood. Four families had been assigned to this small town, located not far from Winnipeg.

Arriving in Homewood, we were struck by the accommodations. Two small houses—lodgings for seasonal workers—sat among the fields. One was a little larger than the other, and two families from Latvia settled into it. Our own little house had one bunkbed covered with an old torn quilt. A thick layer of dust covered the stove and table. We immediately gave our house a name: the kennel. We were terribly thirsty. We found a well in the yard; when we began to pump, we saw that the water was brownish and had a horrible taste.

Since the sugar beets had not yet been planted, there was not a lot of work. The landlady came that first day and took the women to the local grocery store about ten miles away. There she opened an account in her name, so that we could purchase groceries. The time to forget about a hungry existence had come. My God! How we threw ourselves at the huge displays of food! Everyone except for Ivan Nikolaevich began to gain weight.

A week later, our landlady came by with a woman. She asked if any of us women wanted to go work in another farm's household until the sugar beet season started. I was chosen and agreed to go, even though it meant I would be separated from my family.

The woman returned the next day and took me away. Her family were devout German Mennonites. As they spoke the low German dialect, it was sometimes difficult for me to understand them. She began describing the work to be done even before we entered the house. My day began at five o'clock in the morning in the kitchen, preparing breakfast for the family and the workers, who would already be out in the fields on tractors. The workday stretched until ten or eleven at night, the same schedule that I had worked on the farm in Bavaria. I received nine dollars pay each week, which was the first money I earned in Canada.

Toward the end of the week, I could no longer bear to be away from my daughter and asked the landlady to let me go get Anechka. She agreed.

The neighboring farmer needed workers to uproot bushes that he had burned to make more room for planting. On my recommendation, he hired our men, paying them fifty cents an hour. They would return home late in the evening, completely black. But none of us grumbled about the conditions. The main thing was that we were not hungry and there was hope for the future.

"We haven't gone to mother's for a visit," my husband recited the Russian proverb.[5] "We must be patient and work, and all will be well!"

The season for weeding the sugar beets soon began. Each morning we got up at four o'clock. The men went out to the field while I prepared breakfast. At five-thirty, I took the food to them in the field. After quickly gulping it down, they began work again. It was hard labor using the spade to uproot the clumps of grass from the parched, hard earth. I fell ill at the beginning of this season and lay in bed about two weeks, but I forced myself to get up and work.

The humidity and heat were unbearable that summer in Manitoba. The landlady of the neighboring farm often sent her son with a large thermos of cold, clear water. Our own landlady was not concerned about us, and the neighbor openly expressed her indignation about this. There was no indoor plumbing in the houses, and we had to find a way to wash ourselves after twelve to thirteen hours of sweat and dust. We asked the landlady for the pail that was used for watering the kitchen garden and, pumping it full of the rusty water, we helped each other wash, hiding behind the houses.

Our poor clothing quickly wore out, rotted from the sweat and dirt. We had to turn to our landlady again to purchase clothing and underwear on credit. Only my daughter was always clean and well dressed. The neighbor sewed clothing for her own two daughters and two sons. Her children were older than Anechka, and many of their dresses were altered for my daughter. Thus went that first summer in Canada.

Even though we did not work for the neighboring farmers, their warmth toward the workers astonished us. They would look after my daughter during the days and even invited her to stay overnight with them. Anechka quickly learned English from them and often helped us when we did not understand something.

In spite of all the difficulties, we were happy to be in a free country where we would find the path to a better life. Returning home tired in the evenings, my husband still found a moment for humor. This broke the daily monotony and drudgery.

Toward the end of the weeding season, my husband and I began to think about what to do until the time for harvesting the sugar beets arrived in autumn. I offered to go to Winnipeg and search for work. At a family meeting, it was decided that we should ask our landlords for an advance on our wages to pay for my trip. They agreed at once.

I arrived in Winnipeg on a Sunday and immediately went to the church on Manitoba Street, where I met several Russians who subsequently helped me a great deal.

One Russian woman, an émigré from the Pribaltic states named Ekaterina Vladimirovna, worked in a hospital kitchen. She had come to Canada with her grown daughter as a contract worker. Her daughter worked in the laundry at the same hospital. Although her daughter was highly educated and spoke English well, she nevertheless had to fulfill her one-year work contract and work in the laundry. They lived in a garret at the hospital and, as Ekaterina Vladimirovna said, "died from the heat there."

As we were leaving the church, they suggested that I stay with them a few days, and I gratefully accepted.

The next day, after they had both gone to work and I remained in the room alone, someone knocked on the door. I opened it, and before me stood a woman in a white uniform who was obviously a nurse. She examined me from head to toe with malicious eyes. I still understood little English, but I could guess from her tone and gestures that her questions concerned who I was and why I was there. Apparently one of the workers in a neighboring room had reported me to her. She summoned my new acquaintance from work and rebuked her for sheltering me without the administration's permission. Poor Ekaterina Vladimirovna was terribly unsettled. I was even more agitated, for I knew that I was the cause of her predicament.

After work, Ekaterina Vladimirovna treated me to dinner in a restaurant, and we parted company. In those days, Winnipeg was a small city with a large Ukrainian population. Many of the Ukrainians from our camp had gone to Canada before us and ended up in Winnipeg. The difficulty was finding them. Walking down the street, I could hear the Ukrainian language and see Slavic faces everywhere. "A tongue will get you to Kiev,"[6] our people often say truthfully.

While on McGregor Street, I saw the colorful shawls of two old Ukrainian women coming toward me. Stopping them, I asked whether they knew any of the newly arrived Ukrainians. One of the old women happily told me of a family living on Jarvis Street, which had sponsored a relative named Boiko from Germany. I remembered a tailor by that name in our camp. The street was quite near, and I easily found the house in which this Ukrainian man lived. No one was home—everyone was at work. I wandered about the city until five o'clock and returned again to Jarvis Street.

By then everyone was home, and Boiko turned out to be the same man I knew in Germany. His landlady, Madame Melnik, worked in a clothing factory and had found him a job at another plant, finishing the handwork on men's and women's overcoats. Madame Melnik herself sewed at a sportswear factory. She had already worked there a long time and was on good terms with the factory administration.

They invited me to have supper with them. I will never forget the delicious mashed potatoes and *golubtsy*.[7] I told the kind and good-hearted Madame Melnik of my plans to find an apartment and jobs for my husband and me. She immediately suggested I come with her, for she had seen a sign advertising vacant apartments on this same street.

Besides a smattering of older and longtime settlers, most of the residents of this street were Ukrainians or Poles. We later found out that Jarvis Street was among the worst in Winnipeg. Freight trains were always lumbering by noisily on the nearby railroad tracks, spewing soot from the steam engines over the neighborhood day and night. That's where we found an apartment.

It was a medium-sized two-story house, not far from the Melniks' home. The apartment consisted of two rooms, a small kitchen, and a bath on the second floor. There was no furniture at all in our apartment, so the four of us slept on the floor, covering the linoleum with an old tablecloth that Madame Melnik had given me. The landlords were Galician Ukrainians. They shared our bathroom on the second floor.

So a roof had been found to cover our heads, and if we had to sleep on the floor without blankets or pillows, this was not such a great misfortune; Siberia, the camps, and the forced labor in Germany had been worse by far. The next task was to find jobs.

Madame Melnik took me with her to the clothing factory, where I was hired. Only God and I know what terrible indignities I experienced at this factory. My ignorance of the language was one of the main reasons for my humiliation.

A certain female administrator was well known by all the workers for her cruelty and her cynicism. She tried to squeeze all that was possible out of the workers and would fire them on the spot without pity if they raised the least objection. She forced the new workers to work overtime, because they were the worst paid, at thirty-five cents an hour. Fearing to lose the job, I complied with all her demands.

Besides her, the factory's floor manager, an old maid, had no respect for anyone. Her voice reminded me of a turkey's, always yelling, "Hurry up! Hurry up!" This impatient woman had to teach me to use the industrial sewing machine. Although this was the first time in my life that I had set foot in a factory, I tried my best to learn how to sew on this machine.

After four hours of this woman's screaming, she removed me from the machine and handed me a broom. I had to perform all the unskilled labor: sweeping the floors; carrying heavy bundles of trousers, parkas, and men's winter overcoats; and standing for hours at the last position on the conveyor belt, to give the completed garments one last inspection before they were sent off. If a worker began to earn a bit more than the factory wanted to pay per hour, the woman superintendent would immediately cut her proceeds per dozen articles produced.

I worked at the factory for an entire year and said nothing, except to the few other workers who were in a similar position. I bore all this silently, unquestioningly fulfilling all that was demanded of me. After I arrived home exhausted from each day of indignity, however, I let the tears come. I cried a lot, but I hid it all from my family.

One day, a young blonde woman approached me and asked me something in English. I automatically answered her in Russian, saying that I did not understand her question. She was glad that I spoke Russian and began to talk with me in a pure dialect. For a long time she had thought me a Canadian and avoided me. Her name was Katia and her kindness immediately won me over. She and her mother had come from Germany, sponsored by relatives. Her father had

been a Russian-born German but had died in prison during
the Stalin purges. Her mother had been fired from her job as a
designer since she was the wife of an "enemy of the people."
Unable to find a job, her mother had moved from the city to
a collective farm to save her three children from a hungry
death. After we got to know each other, Katia often came to
my defense. Whenever someone at the factory tried to treat
me badly, she immediately intervened.

When our Russian colony in Winnipeg arranged parties, I took her with me. Since we could not afford evening
dresses, we decided to make them ourselves. We bought
black velvet, not knowing that such material could only be
cut in one direction. Our dresses came out darker in front
than in back. We both laughed, but went to the dance nevertheless.

Katia was a kindhearted soul, sensitive to everyone's
needs. She respected and loved me, and I paid her in kind.
In her I saw another daughter. I often tried to inspire her,
explaining how it was necessary to fight for life while keeping
dignity and honor. Our family shared both sorrow and joy
with her.

We worked together for only two years before she left
to get married, but our good friendship continues to this day.
Katia married a professor from Manitoba University, and
they have two children. Their daughter became a doctor, and
their son took a great interest in music.

My position at the factory gradually improved. I finally learned to use all kinds of machines and through my
conduct earned the respect of the administration and the
workers. After two years, I was chosen as union representative, often defending wronged workers. I had frequent
clashes with the head administrator of the factory over unfair
treatment of employees. Sometimes she and I would not
speak to each other for entire weeks.

When we were speaking, I would implore her to consider the factory workers as people rather than as numbers.
I argued that considering them as people with equal rights
would raise production. On many occasions when she dis-
missed older workers, I would intervene, and they would be

restored to their jobs, sometimes even with a raise in pay. We gradually became friends.

3

I remained as union representative at the clothing factory for more than fourteen years, until I left to pursue further education at Manitoba University. I attended evening classes, after putting in ten or eleven hours per day at the factory. It was the factory's policy to keep me working as many hours as possible, so that I would not have time left for studies. The factory owner himself did not want to lose me and tried to persuade me not to overtire myself with study.

"Why do you want to go to the university?" he would ask me. "I don't have a higher education . . . all those I went to school with are now doctors or lawyers, but all of them admire me—I'm a millionaire!"

Throughout my life, I had always set a goal and striven with persistence to achieve it. My dream was to earn a Western teaching degree. My yearning to work in the profession I adored enabled me to overcome all barriers except for one: an insufficient knowledge of English. I was proficient only in factory jargon, words and phrases concerning bundles or lot numbers. Physical effort during the long days at the factory and mental effort during my studies in the evenings challenged me to the limits of my strength.

I studied at Manitoba University for two semesters, and the professors in the Slavic Department, especially the department head, began to advise me to go to the United States for summer courses.

"There is an open road before you, but only in the USA. Here in Canada, you won't be given the chance. The Ukrainians won't allow a Russian to become an instructor here," a professor who himself was Ukrainian told me.

I discussed this option with my daughter, who was now twenty-two and working for an insurance company, and my husband. Both enthusiastically began to urge me to submit an application for admission to summer school. I hesitated, and not without reason. First, we hadn't the money and, second, I dreaded that my husband, playing poker, would lose everything, including our house. His passion for card playing was ruining us. He provided me with much moral support, however, and when I missed the deadline for submitting the application, he even stopped speaking to me, in protest.

"How can you have been so foolish?" he scolded me. "You have what it takes to achieve your goal!"

"Yes, maybe I do have what it takes," I answered. "But not the money!"

We decided to borrow the money, and I sent my application to Middlebury College late, knowing that there was little hope of being accepted. A few days later, the director of the Russian School at Middlebury College called with the wonderful news that my application for admission into the Russian program had been accepted.

The prospect of a ten-week course in a strange country frightened me. I also was reluctant to leave my family for such a long time and to go into debt. It was too late to retreat from the decision, however, and there was only one route—forward.

In the beginning of June 1962, I flew to Montreal and traveled by bus to Vermont from there. Representatives of the Russian Department met arriving students at the bus station in Middlebury. Among the arriving students were also professors who were to teach in the Russian program. At first I was taken for a professor. "No, I'm only a student!" I would reply.

When we arrived, we registered for the courses and found our assigned rooms. In my dormitory, the resident professor was Madame Ekaterina Vladimirovna Volkonskaia. This dear woman, a great friend to her students, had a great deal of teaching experience. She was an excellent professor. I also met Professor Elena Aleksandrovna Scriabine there. Speaking for the Arts Department, she asked me whether I would participate in the annual play.

"I've come to take classes, not to be in a play," I answered.

I was hardly able to finish before the director of the

Russian School walked up. Elena Aleksandrovna told him that I had refused to take a part in the play. After a stern lecture from him, I agreed to participate.

My association with Elena Aleksandrovna changed the direction of my life, for she persuaded me to apply to graduate school at the University of Iowa, where she was a valued professor of Russian language and literature, during the academic year.

During my first semester in Iowa, I was offered a position as a teaching assistant. I taught Russian language to beginning students. On my first day, I went to class fearfully, not knowing American students well. By the next day, however, I was gladly hurrying to class. I had about 130 students in three classes. I loved seeing their serious faces, striving to learn a difficult language.

Besides my teaching duties, I had to take the courses required for the master's degree. I received my diploma after three semesters and was offered a full-time teaching position as instructor of Russian language. This was the happy year of 1967!

My daughter flew from Canada for the triumph of my graduation from the University of Iowa. Her eyes shone with joy at her mother's success. "I was sure that you would reach your goal, Mamochka. You're a fighter, and an example to me of how to reach my own goal" were her exact words.

Now it was time to find a teaching position, so that my lifelong dream could be realized. "I can keep you here at the University of Iowa, but you would always be a student in the eyes of your former professors," advised Dean Stuit. "Consider offers from other universities. I will give you the very best recommendation."

After interviews with the representatives of three universities, I was offered the opportunity to move to California. At first, I had been ready to accept a contract in Wisconsin, but under my daughter's pressure, I decided to accept the offer of California State University, Fresno. It was a good decision.

My husband and daughter were still in Canada, and I had to live without them for three-and-a-half years, until they received permission to be permanent residents of the

United States. Ivan Nikolaevich never really wanted to leave Canada, even though the cold climate endangered his health. In addition, his frequent sleepless nights playing cards were destroying his already bad heart. But he came with Anechka anyway.

I was constantly busy with work. In the Department of Foreign Languages, many of my colleagues extended to me the hand of friendship. I participated actively in a woman's club, whose members were professors and staff from all departments.

Anechka married and settled in southern California, where she still works for an insurance company. My husband, remaining home alone, pined for Canada, his friends, and even for his former job, though it had been hard and physical. He longed to return to Canada, if only for a short time. I was against this idea, fearing that it was only his yearning for a card game. I later became convinced that I was wrong, for it was morally hard for him to accept being without friends and dependent on his wife.

I enjoyed my work, my home, and my family for thirteen years. All of life moves in cycles, however. Fortune smiles, and then dark clouds cover its gleam.

Ivan Nikolaevich's health took a sharp turn for the worse. He suffered his first heart attack in 1965, but quickly recovered and continued to work. Moving to the warm climate of California prolonged his life by a few years, but he became unbelievably erratic and demanding. Anything, no matter how trivial, irritated him. I tried to satisfy all his whims and ease his suffering.

When the doctor first detected a distention of the aorta in his chest and proposed an operation, my husband categorically refused. I tried to convince him otherwise, but he said only that he was thankful for having been able to live so long.

"After all, I could have been shot," he argued. "I could have perished in a *kontslager'* or as a prisoner of the Germans, but I survived all that."

He continued, "I was destined to meet you, my dear, and to live all these years. Really, isn't that good fortune? You have been for me that bright ray, and thanks to you I was able to endure all manner of humiliations. I want you never to doubt my love for you. I have often been unfair to you, knowing full well that you did not deserve to be hurt. I kept none of my promises concerning card games. I saw that you and our daughter tolerated all my mischief."

"I tolerated everything because I valued your love for Anechka and, second, I never allowed myself thoughts of divorce," I told Ivan Nikolaevich, pushing aside my personal hurt.

My mother's teachings had made the notion of divorce unacceptable in my family's traditions. Reflecting on the past, however, I think that such a view of life may not be completely fair. My own brother was compelled to live with a wife who was unfaithful to him, and when his thoughts turned to divorce, our mother admonished, "There have been no divorces in all our family." Although I had to bear treatment that I did not deserve, I do not complain that I was a victim. To the end, I carried out my duty as a wife, which I had vowed to do at the time of the wedding ceremony.

With each passing day, Ivan Nikolaevich grew weaker. He simply wasted away before my eyes. Both of us saw his approaching death, but said nothing. He finally agreed to the bypass operation, but it was too late. The heart specialist sadly informed me that Ivan Nikolaevich's condition was hopeless. How hard it was for me to hear this, and harder still to explain it to my husband!

He very bravely heard me out and only said, "Well, then, take me home. I want to die at home."

Meanwhile, my daughter had made arrangements for him to see a specialist in southern California. On the day he was to go, we were on the way to the airport. I had not even turned the corner when he began to breathe rapidly and fell from the seat. I went directly to the hospital.

I burst out of the car and into the building, shouting that my husband was dying in the car. With the speed of lightning, they came out of the emergency room and brought him in. He was already unconscious, but still alive.

I was not allowed to see him at first. After a little while I went in, and he began to speak to me. They took him by elevator up to the cardiography room. I held his hand in the elevator. With a smile on his face, he spoke his last words to me.

"Farewell, Lenochka, this is the end. I am ready to go to the other world. Only one thing troubles me: that you will suffer without me."

"Oh, no, don't tell me that," I answered him, holding back sobs.

That was our last conversation. A half hour later he left me forever. The last page in the life of a man—cast by fate into a country of which he had never dreamed, but in which he found freedom—was closed on February 2, 1980.

Those who pass to the other world are relieved of physical and mental suffering, but those who are left behind undergo torment, having lost their dear ones. Such is the way of the world, such is our fate, and no one can avoid it.

Epilogue

So I am again alone. I live with the past, in which there was more bitterness than happiness. But forgetting the past would mean not finding pleasure in the present.

The light of my life is my beloved daughter and her family. Whenever I am feeling terribly lonely, I think of her. Loneliness is especially palpable when I am not working at the university. The students and their shining faces take the place of the long-lost family and relatives of whose fates I know nothing. The greatest joy for me is working with the younger generation. I share with my students not only the knowledge of the subjects I teach, but also the experience of what I have survived. I force my students to think about questions concerning the reality that surrounds us.

Most of my students do not know hunger and deprivation. They have no conception of life without any freedom. What good fortune they enjoy! This explains why so many immigrants who have come to this country are fully satisfied with life, regardless of some difficulties in adjusting to the customs of the society.

One of my personal characteristics is that I never complain. I have always believed that there is a way out of any difficult situation, and no work, be it physical or mental, has ever frightened me. While labor can bring material success, the most important elements in life are respect and love for those around us.

If I treat people kindly, perhaps someone will do the same for my relatives wherever they may be. I lost my parents long ago, but have maintained indelible memories of them and their suffering. As a result, whenever I meet elderly or helpless people, I am always the first to extend a helping hand. Older people prepared the ground for our lives, and we should never forget that. Without the past there can be no present, and without the present there can be no future. Such is my outlook on life.

Faith in God is the force that saved me from death and eased my spiritual torments. To serve those near to you is to serve God. I am happy to live in a country where the word "God" is not forbidden.

NOTES

JOURNEY THROUGH TORMENT

1. An administrative region of the Soviet Union.
2. Administrative districts in the Soviet Union.
3. A worker "richer" than other peasants was seen as a threat to the establishment of socialism.
4. Cheka was the state police organization.
5. The NKVD was predecessor to the KGB (Committee for State Security).
6. The Kirghiz, one of the minorities in the Soviet Union, are a people of the Turkic language group.
7. *Kolkhoz* means collective farm.
8. Hobos and members of the criminal element.
9. The Civil War began after the 1917 October Revolution. Members of the White Army were defenders of the old tsarist system. The Red Army, headed by Lenin, opposed them.

A RAY OF HAPPINESS

1. An eighteenth-century physical chemist and poet who laid the foundations of the modern Russian literary language.
2. A district in the south of Leningrad.
3. An instructor of political ideology.
4. "Stalin school" was the general term for schools (mostly secondary schools) built during his reign.

SHORTLIVED JOY

1. *Vy* is the formal form of address used as a sign of respect. *Ty* is used with close friends or family.
2. The Civil Registrar's Office, where marriages are registered.
3. A Russian toast meaning the drinks are bitter but that the kisses of the bride and groom will sweeten them.
4. A long sleeveless gown.
5. Supporters of Lev Davidovich Trotsky, who was exiled from the Soviet Union and subsequently murdered by Stalin's agents in Mexico.
6. Joachim von Ribbentrop and Vyacheslav Mikhailovich Molotov, Soviet and German ministers of foreign affairs, had signed a nonaggression pact in 1939.
7. Voroshilov was Soviet commander of the northwest armies.
8. Russian given name, here referring generically to all Russians.

SORROWFUL STRUGGLES

1. *Kolkhoznik* means collective farmer.
2. "Registrants," or those who had retreated from the Germans and taken refuge elsewhere to avoid fighting. These people, most of whom were in the military, had to register with the authorities when they came to live in a village, although many did not. They often remained in the village by marrying into a local family.
3. "Gendarmerie" was a Soviet term for the German police.
4. Often translated as *The Possessed*.
5. Deep pits that had formerly been underground silos of the collective farms.
6. Concentration camps.

TORN FROM THE MOTHERLAND

1. A *trinozhka* is a small three-legged stand on which pots and pans are placed and under which a fire is built.
2. A character in Russian folktales.
3. "Watch out!"
4. *Arbeitsdienst* means work service.
5. *Ostovtsy* means people from Eastern Europe or the Soviet Union.
6. *Kontslagerniki* means people who are or have been in *kontslageria* or concentration camps.
7. The first emigration took place following the Russian Civil War and World War I.
8. Andrei Andreevich Vlasov, a Soviet captured by the Germans early in the war, fought with them against the Soviet Union to overthrow Stalin.
9. Marshal of the Soviet Union and Chief of Staff Mikhail Nikolaevich Tukhachevskii and seven other commanders were arrested in June 1937 on charges of collaborating with Germany.
10. A colloquial way to address a man as "sir."
11. *Sovetchiki* means representatives of the Soviet Repatriation Mission.

FREEDOM FOUND

1. The man responsible for the people in the barracks.
2. Wladyslaw Anders (1892–1970) fought with the Russian Army during World War I, then against the Red Army in the Russo-Polish War of 1919–1920. At the beginning of World War II, he fought against both Germany and the Soviet Union, until he was captured and imprisoned by the Soviets. When Germany and the Soviet Union went to war, he was released and formed a fighting force of former prisoners of war and deportees, which was under Soviet control. As such, Anders could not fight to free Poland; under Polish and British pressure, his army was allowed to campaign in Iran, Iraq, and

Italy. In 1945, the Polish government-in-exile, in London, named him commander-in-chief of the Polish Army. A staunch anti-Communist, Anders remained in Great Britain after the end of the war and, in 1946, was deprived of his citizenship by the new Communist Polish government. He was a prominent leader of Polish exiles in the West until his death.

3. From "Conceived in night, I was born into night . . ." by Aleksandr Aleksandrovich Blok.
4. That is, let the grass grow under my feet.
5. That is, things weren't going to be easy.
6. That is, you can find your way by asking.
7. Cabbage leaves filled with various mixtures of meat or rice and cooked.